Arts: A Third Level Course

The Development of Instruments and their Music
Units 4–6

Baroque Instrumental Music 1
People, Instruments and the Continuo

Prepared by Owain Edwards for the Course Team

The Open University Press

49347

The Open University Press,
Walton Hall, Milton Keynes.

First published 1974.

Designed by the Media Development Group of the Open University.

Printed in Great Britain by
Martin Cadbury, a specialized division of Santype International,
Worcester and London.

ISBN 0 335 00852 6

This text forms part of an Open University course. The complete list of units in the course appears at the end of this text.

For general availability of supporting material referred to in this text, please write to the Director of Marketing, The Open University, P.O. Box 81, Walton Hall, Milton Keynes, MK7 6AA.

Further information on Open University courses may be obtained from the Admissions Office, The Open University, P.O. Box 48, Walton Hall, Milton Keynes, MK7 6AA.

CONTENTS

You will have gathered from the foregoing study of the organ and its music, that the Baroque period was musically one of innovation and expansion. I want to pay attention now to music for the other instruments, which were often played in ensemble with the organ, in particular those of the emerging violin family. From what is a vast and crowded scene it will be our task to trace out the important lines of development, while trying also to gain a fair overall impression of Baroque instrumental music.

The material is presented in two parts. In units 4–6 I make a general introduction to the scene, look at the musical instruments individually, and discuss the matter of the *basso continuo*. Units 7–9 are mainly concerned with the historical development of the three forms of instrumental composition most commonly used in the period: the suite, the sonata and the concerto. We are going to concentrate primarily on identifying the stylistic characteristics of Baroque music, through analysis of pieces which we have on record. Focusing attention on these particular pieces ought to help increase your skill as a listener of music in general. The long-term gain which you might well recognize after having taken this course could be that you find you derive more satisfaction from concerts that you attend, and are more fully aware of what is going on in the music.

The rate at which you get through the work will naturally depend on your knowledge, abilities and interest. You might bear in mind here and throughout the course, that since music scores take up some of the units in each block (units 10–11 in our case) the amount of work represented by the printed unit is consistently rather more than a week of your time.

These units have been prepared by Owain Edwards who gratefully acknowledges helpful discussions with colleagues in the faculty.

Assignments

There are two Tutor Marked Assignments for these units on Baroque Instrumental Music. The first should be completed in week seven, the second in the final week of the block. Please consult the Course Guide for the dates by which they should be submitted to your Tutor.

Set texts

In addition to *Musical Instruments through the Ages* edited by Anthony Baines (Penguin Books, 1961) and Arthur Jacobs *A New Dictionary of Music* (Penguin Books, 1958), which you'll already have used, you will need to make reference to two miniature scores: Corelli, *Concerto Grosso op. 6 no. 8* 'The Christmas Concerto', and Vivaldi, *Concerto Grosso op. 3 no. 8*, both in Eulenberg's edition.

Records

Make sure you have Baroque Music II and III before starting on this block. You are not required to buy any additional records; all the relevant musical illustrations you will need are included on these.

The Broadcasts

Full details of the four radio and four television programmes in this block are given in the Broadcast Supplement. In each case it would be very helpful if you made a point of reading the notes on the programme beforehand. It is so much easier to remember the point of a programme if you know what you are looking for in it. When we are concerned with now obsolete musical instruments 'efficient' viewing of a television programme clearly is imperative. We have assumed that the programmes at the beginning of the block will be reinforcing material you will already have digested rather than are receiving for the first time.

Aims and objectives of the block

Taking the main aim of the course, that of tracing the development of musical instruments and of the music composed for them, we concentrate here on the period extending roughly from 1600 to 1750. So much was happening in the Baroque period that I could not attempt to cover adequately each development of interest or significance in instrument building or in instrumental music. I do attempt nevertheless a general survey in order to emphasize the developments in musical form as well as the technological advances in instrument making that, with the advantage of hindsight, we know to have been important.

To a point, one can learn about the instruments by reading and listening. No amount of reading or listening, however, will make one comprehend accurately the technical difficulties which a virtuoso performer overrides with apparent ease. The music must be viewed in a historical context, but studying it requires getting involved in it intellectually and emotionally too. As you read these earlier units of the block, I hope you will be gaining a view of aspects of musical life in the Baroque era, a historical perspective to which you will be able to relate the music itself.

Abbreviations

The titles of books which are referred to frequently in these units are abbreviated for convenience. A list of the abbreviations may be found on page 128.

Portrait of Vivaldi in Liceo Musicale G. B. Martini, Bologna (Fotofast)

6

2 PEOPLE AND PLACES

2.1 The Age of the Violin

The Baroque era has been called the age of the violin, the age of Italian opera, and of itinerant Italian virtuosi.

What was it that warrants associating the Baroque particularly with the violin? This was the time of Corelli, Vivaldi, Bach and Handel, but who were their lesser contemporaries, and how strongly did they feel the influence of Corelli and the great composers of the period? What kind of music was composed and who played it? Where, and who paid for it? How was it played, and what did it sound like?

I hope that you will have a clear idea of the answer both to these and more questions about Baroque music before you finish working through these units. You ought by then to have become reasonably familiar with the characteristics of this kind of music, and with increased familiarity will probably be enjoying listening to it with greater understanding. If you do, there is positive gain from taking the trouble to learn what is of historical and analytical interest about it. Apart from the fact that becoming aware of the subtleties can be an absorbing subject in itself, the way you feel emotionally about a piece may be enhanced if you also happen to know how music of that kind was usually written, how your particular piece differs from the conventional and from other such pieces by the same composer, how it was received at the time, how it is constructed, how this performance you are listening to compares with that, and so on. The pleasure you get from listening to the Baroque music we have on record and in the broadcasts ought to be enriched through greater familiarity with the life of the period. As you read you have an opportunity to learn enough about the musical scene and its conventions to see why certain lines of development are of relevance while others are not, and from gaining a general view of instrumental music at the time I hope you will appreciate how Corelli and a few others distinguish themselves from their fellow musicians.

Why is the Baroque often called the age of the violin, when violins were being made before this period, back in the sixteenth century? The reason is that it was in the seventeenth and eighteenth centuries, in music of the Baroque style, that the violin really came into its own. The period saw first the violin and viola displacing the smallest members of the viol family, not only in dance music for which they were considered obviously superior, and in that latest Italian invention opera, for which their volume and attack were valued, but also gradually in all kinds of music-making. More and more the cello and double bass were also found preferable to the 'lower' viols, the viola da gamba and the violone. Writing in his *General History of Music* (1789) the English historian Charles Burney, to whose observations we shall have frequent recourse, comments facetiously on the

> great progress which the *violin tribe* had made towards perfection, about the middle of the last century. The celebrity and importance which this family has acquired, since it may be said to have *got up* in the world, and made so much noise every where, may excite curiosity in its admirers about its manner of *going on*, and *passing its time*, one hundred and thirty years ago, before its offspring had contrived to be invited as pleasant and necessary companions in all places of ceremony, festivity and amusement. The disposition of the several orders and ranks of this fraternity . . . in the infancy of their state, was the following: *Violino primo, Violino secondo, Alto,*

and *Basso di Viola*; an order that is still continued in their private, as well as public meetings, which may afford some satisfaction to curious enquirers into family-compacts. And it must appear somewhat singular, that though many of this race are of a gigantic size, yet the *great* usually submit to be *led* and governed by the *small*, in every congress or muster, be their numbers ever so considerable.[1]

This period saw the northern Italian schools of violin-making raise the instrument to perfection—the Cremonese school, notably the Amati and Guarneri families and Antonio Stradivari, being particularly important—and it saw the emergence of equally influential schools of composition and playing.

The perfecting of the violin as an efficient instrument, beautiful to look at and listen to, was inseparably associated with the progress of violin playing and of the particular forms of composition which naturally developed to accommodate it most sympathetically: the sonata and the concerto.

From our modern vantage-point it is too easy to be unaware of the importance of the seventeenth-century Italian virtuosi of the violin. One has little idea of the standard of technical competence at that time unless one makes a point of finding out by listening and reading about it. We have all heard of Paganini though, and the stereotype of virtuosity on the violin is tied up with Paganini-like performances of Romantic violin music consisting of thousands of notes a minute, played at incredible speed, covering a range in excess of four octaves— and past this nineteenth-century barrier our conventional musical background doesn't assist us in finding the necessary way.

Only a small fraction of the music actually played in the seventeenth and eighteenth centuries is heard with any frequency today, and most of it dates from the early eighteenth century, the period of Bach, Handel and Vivaldi, which saw the final stage in the development of the Baroque sonata and concerto. The mature product in this style of writing is generally preferred to the experimental essays of its early days. Consequently we seldom have an opportunity to judge the success of the compositions and observe the degree of technical virtuosity exhibited in the sonatas of Biagio Marini (c. 1597–1665) for example, Marco Uccellini (c. 1603–80) and Giovanni Legrenzi (1627–90), foremost amongst early Italians in their treatment of form and violin technique, or of Carlo Farina (c. 1600–c.40) who, settling in Dresden in 1625, literally showed the Germans what was possible on the violin. Only infrequently (and in the spirit of open-minded missionary work) is the prodigiously difficult violin music of the Austrian Heinrich Biber (1644–1704) included in recitals, and even less do we hear that of his equally demanding contemporary J. J. Walther (c. 1650–1717).

That it was the age of the violin is well illustrated by the number of musicians, Italians mostly, who made a livelihood teaching the violin or performing on it. They provided the guidance and expertise sought by a willing and enthusiastic musical public. So much were the Italians in evidence in London, for example, during the early eighteenth century, that although their services were not completely indispensable, to have withdrawn them might have led to a collapse of the city's musical activities. London, incidentally, was regarded by foreign musicians as a profitable base for activities. At a rough estimate at least eighty Italians worked in the city from the late seventeenth century to 1750, and Germans too came in increasing numbers following the accession of the House of Hanover in 1714. Nor was London exceptional in its capacity to provide

[1] *BH*, ii, 435.

work and opportunities to so many Italians. Over the same period, Vienna took in more than a hundred, St Petersburg about twenty-five, Dresden, forty, and Paris in the region of fifty.[1]

What opportunities were available to be competed for by native musicians and by the inevitable itinerant Italians? They varied quite a lot from country to country.

France

In France professional music was concentrated almost entirely on the court at Versailles and the opera in Paris. In the seventeenth century the nation's musical dictator was the brilliant Florentine emigré, known by the naturalized form of his name, Jean-Baptiste Lully (1632–87).

The most fortunate musicians (since positions were often hereditary) attained appointments in one of the three royal musical establishments: the Chapel (and either of the two 'secular' establishments), the Chamber and the Ecurie. In the Chamber were two orchestras, whose function was to provide any kind of music the king wished for his entertainment. The older and more famous was the *Grande Bande* or 'Twenty-four violins of the King'. The other, *Les Petits Violons*, was the orchestra whose playing Charles II, after his exile in France, tried to emulate with his own 'Private Musick' in England. Besides these, there were also players of plucked instruments, wind players and singers (in the Chamber). The other secular establishment, the Ecurie, was a full band with oboes, bassoons, trumpets, drums and instruments of the bagpipe family in addition to the strings. They worked as a ceremonial band, performing either mounted or on foot. When necessary for large-scale occasions, the strength of the Chapel was reinforced by musicians from the Chamber and Ecurie. All in all it was a closed circle which, as you will see when we consider the development of the sonata, had its disadvantages. 'Outside', however, the Royal Academy of Music provided an independent outlet which after the death of Louis XIV in 1715 was increasingly influential.[2]

Court musicians were most frequently engaged in playing dance music. While the wide range of current French dances required a particular expertise in the way they should be performed, they demanded only a moderate competence in actual violin technique. French influence during the Baroque era is thus felt in matters of style, not in the advancement of technique. The French school of violin playing rose to importance, however, towards the end of the eighteenth century and continued through the nineteenth to be the dominant school of violin playing.

Apart from the style—the French way of performing their kind of music which was in itself very influential—there was something else which in the long run was to find permanence in the music of composers outside France. The so-called French Overture was a form which probably every composer of instrumental music adopted in the period starting with the first example by Lully in his ballet *Alcidiane* (1658), and ending with the demise of the Baroque style in the middle of the following century.

Exercise

Listen to the overture to Lully *Le Divertissement de Chambord* which is on record. No score is provided in units 10–11 of this introductory movement to Lully's

[1] *The Larousse Encyclopedia of Music* (Hamlyn, London, 1971), 208.

[2] *Ibid.*, 221.

'Entertainment at Chambord', his setting of music to Molière's 'Monsieur de Pourceaugnac'. In this overture are the characteristic features which composers included as essentials of the French Overture, although the proportions were subsequently modified.

1 It falls into a number of sections marked by distinct tempi, texture and meter. How many sections?

2 Indicate with the help of a diagram the proportions of the movement. Then add to it details of the tempo and the number of beats in the bar in each section.

3 Say what you listen to in particular in each section: is it the melody, a distinctive rhythm, the harmony?

4 Finally, and more difficult: could the various sections make effective separate movements, are they each self-contained, beginning and ending convincingly in the same key?

Play Baroque Music III side 1 band 1

My Comments

1 Two

2

Slow   *Fast*
4 beats   *6 quick beats or 2 slower ones.*

3 I don't listen particularly to the melody in the first section, my attention is taken more by the rich harmony and texture, and by the strong rhythmic figure ♩.. ♪ and the fuller ♩. ♪♪♪♪ which presses persistently onward. I listen to the melody in the fast section and find it interesting to follow it as it is played in various parts, now on the top, now below.

4 The second could, although being only thirty-five seconds long it is on the short side to stand alone. The opening section could not, because it does not end with a conclusive cadence. Instead the music comes to rest on the dominant chord, implying that it has to go on, which it does.

Further Comment

The two sections of this particular movement show the distinguishing elements of the French overture. The slow but energetic opening, often rich in harmony and texture, and massive in effect in which the rhythm identified above is always strongly evident, and the faster fugal section following it. In some French overtures there is a return to the opening material after the fugal section, thus making a slow-fast-slow arrangement. Both the two and three-section forms of French overture were commonly used and the proportions of the sections in relation to one another varied considerably: some composers emphasizing the slow sections, others investing the fugal section with the greatest interest and even exceeding the slow sections in playing time.

Germany

In the conglomeration of German-speaking states any King, Prince, Elector or Landgrave with musical leanings and the necessary wealth to support them might set up musical establishments which provided work for up to twenty and more musicians. An indication of the size of such establishments follows in the closing section of these units. The direction of the court music was in the care of the Kapellmeister, who would be expected to provide music to order and to direct performances of it, usually playing the organ or harpsichord himself, and the Konzertmeister, leader and solo violinist. In the larger establishments, such as those of the King of Poland and Elector of Saxony at Dresden, the King of Prussia at Berlin, the imperial Chapel Royal in Vienna and, from the second quarter of the eighteenth century, the musically brilliant court of the Elector Palatine at Mannheim, the best instrumentalists competed for the most lucrative posts but learned from each other in matters of style and technique, both in performance and composition.

Opera, and theatre music in the form of popular songs and dances, also needed a considerable supply of players, and for these professionals there were opportunities to teach and play in amateur music groups (such as the student music society called the *Collegium Musicum* that Telemann founded whilst he was a student at Leipzig), and on large-scale festive occasions, of playing in church.

Collegium Musicum, Thun 1737 (Bernisches Historisches Museum)

Exercise

As an example of one of the many kinds of music played both at court and in amateur music societies, listen now to the Polonaise from J. S. Bach *Suite in B minor for Flute and Strings*. Again, do this exercise by listening, although later we shall be referring to the score in unit 11. The Polonaise was one of the less common dance movements of the Baroque suite.

1 How many beats are there in a bar?

2 Listen carefully to the rhythm of the opening melody (♫♫♪   ), then count how many times you hear this repeated during the first section, i.e. until there is an obvious change of instrumentation and texture.

3 In the second section, identify the instruments involved. Which plays the tune. How are the others contributing?

4 From this what can you assume about the eighteenth-century flute?

Play Baroque Music III side 1 band 2

My Comments

1 Three.

2 16. Now refer to the score. The rhythm is repeated in bars 1, 2, 3, 5, 6, 9, 10 and 11.

3 Flute, cello, harpsichord. The cello has the Polonaise tune. He is given harmonic support by the harpsichord. The flute plays a counterpoint to the tune.

4 That the instrument was agile, capable of rhythmic accentuation, and loud enough to be heard against a body of strings and harpsichord.

Italy

Music in Italy was fostered with equal enthusiasm in the church and in secular establishments. Opera, which after it had become public for the first time at Venice in 1637 was to provide a livelihood to an increasing number of orchestral players in resident companies in most large cities as well as in travelling groups, was 'invented' in Florence in the courts of Counts Bardi and Corsi during the closing years of the sixteenth century. The marked rise in the production of violins and the spread of proficiency in violin-playing in the seventeenth century saw orchestras formed in many of the larger cathedrals and ecclesiastical establishments—such as St Mark's Cathedral, Venice, and at the enormous Basilica of St Petronio, Bologna. Orchestras played at private courts as well. Corelli, for example, led the music at the celebrated court of Cardinal Ottoboni in Rome, when he was not playing in the opera or taking one of his apparently innumerable pupils on the violin. Almost every Italian virtuoso in the eighteenth century claimed to have been taught by Corelli, incidentally, a claim which could not have been true for all of them but which did a lot to help each of them personally as well as increasing Corelli's tremendous prestige. Important as the places where the sonata and concerto were raised were the music meetings of the aristocratic academies.

> Private music-meetings in Italy were generally organized by the academies which sprang up in every town; these were mainly literary and philo-

sophical societies, but their meetings often included some performance of music. Their membership was generally confined to the nobility and the clergy. It is from these institutions that the word *accademia*—more correctly, *accademia di musica*—came in the days of Dr Burney to signify a concert. The clergy, in addition to the part which they took in the life of the Academies, were often staunch supporters of music in their churches and in their monasteries and convents, which prospered exceedingly under the Spanish dominion. The congregations were often possessed of great wealth and their members enjoyed both comfort and liberty.

Most writers on Italian literature have made fun of the academies, and, above all, of the famous Arcadian Academy at Rome; but when one studies the history of literary and musical effort in the smaller cities of Italy, one cannot help coming to the conclusion that, after the magnificent era of the Renaissance princes had closed, it was very largely the despised Academies which kept culture alive throughout the troublous times when Italian territories were being disputed by the French, the Spaniards, and the Austrians. War or pestilence might suppress for a time the actual meetings of an academy, but its memory remained alive, and as soon as peace was re-established it could collect its scattered members and start its activities afresh.

This account is taken from Edward J. Dent's introduction to a book about violin-makers of the Guarneri family, and since the northern Italian cities of Cremona, Mantua and Venice were associated with the work of members of this famous family he refers to the history of the academies of these three cities. A similar account might be drawn, however, for the academies of other cities, differing only in detail from the one which follows of the activities at Mantua.

The chief academy of Mantua was that of the *Invaghiti*, a society of noblemen under the direct patronage of the Gonzagas and holding its meetings in the ducal palace itself. It was at a private meeting of this body that Monteverdi's *Orfeo*[1] was first performed on February 24th, 1607. The *Invaghiti* dated from 1564. There existed also a less socially exclusive academy, known first as the *Invitti* and later as the *Timidi*. The *Invitti* came to a temporary end at the sack of Mantua in 1630, but a few survivors reconstituted the academy in 1643, and in 1645 the Duke (Charles de Nevers) took them under his protection. They had at that time thirty members. It was in 1648 that they changed their name to the *Timidi*. For sixty years they lived in prosperity; their amalgamation with the academy of the *Imperfetti* in 1689 enabled them to enlarge their theatre, in which they held their literary meetings, gave concerts, and even performed operas of which both words and music were written by their own members. At the beginning of the eighteenth century they collapsed again, but reappeared in 1737, after the termination of the war of the Polish Succession. Although originally a society of middle-class people, they were now joined by a considerable secession from the aristocratic *Invaghiti*. The survivors of the *Invaghiti* became in 1748 a 'colony' of the Arcadians, who about this time were absorbing the smaller and older academies in many parts of Italy. It was obviously an advantage for men of letters and musicians to be able to belong to the same corporation wherever they might happen to travel in Italy; but we may get some idea of the honour in which these older bodies had been held from the fact that the Empress Maria Theresa, in her dispatch to the *Colonia Virgiliana* (as the Mantuan

---

[1] Monteverdi's first opera, and one of the most important of all the early operas.

branch of Arcadia was now called), which she took under her protection in 1752, recommended the new Arcadians to abide as far as possible by the constitutions of the former *Invaghiti*, though it is surprising to find the Austrian Empress taking so much interest in an institution founded by the dispossessed dynasty of the Gonzagas two centuries before. What eventually happened was that in 1767 Maria Theresa united both Academies in one, which still exists and flourishes as the *Accademia Virgiliana*. This body in 1769 absorbed an *Accademia Filarmonica* which had been started by some musical amateurs in 1761. A new theatre was built by Bibbiena and opened on December 3rd, 1769; the third meeting which took place there was the concert given by the young Mozart on the 16th of January 1770.[1]

Members of an academy who were composers naturally provided much of the music for their own use. Sometimes they dedicated their publications to the academy as well. Of the composers whose music was more widely played, none stood in higher renown during the late seventeenth century than Corelli. Although his concertos were not published in his lifetime they became known from the 1680s, circulating in manuscript copies. Corelli shows in his concertos a sensitive awareness of the technical competence of the players normally available. To see this, turn now to the opening movements of his *Concerto Grosso op. 6 no. 8* 'The Christmas Concerto', and after listening (without reference to the score) to about four minutes of it,

Exercise

1 describe the forces involved,

2 comment on how they are deployed.

Play Baroque Music III side 1 band 4

My Comments

1 The music is for string orchestra with organ. The violins are divided as is customary now. We hear them crossing frequently as first the one group of violins is uppermost and then the other is. In the long fast movement two violins, a 'cello and, faintly, the organ stand out as a group of soloists.

2 In the opening movement the strings are used as a single body, but in the fast movement there is an alternation between the soloists and the rest of the orchestra. In fact, it is not strictly a case of first the solo group and then the others although it sounds like this. The soloists play right through and are joined by the others for certain phrases.

We shall be looking more closely at the style and form of this concerto again, but here note that with this choice of parts, Corelli could give the solo players the most difficult music and the less competent members of the academy the 'joining in' parts.

2.2 The First Public Concerts

There was nothing directly comparable to the Italian academy in England, but the music club and the public concert were to serve much the same function, in providing opportunities for musicians to play together and a means by which

[1] William H. Hill, Arthur F. Hill and Alfred E. Hill, *The Violin-makers of the Guarneri family (1626–1762)* (The Holland Press Ltd., London, 1965), xxv–xxvii.

Mr John Bannister,
engraved by Ridley. Doubtful
authenticity (London
Museum)

those who had tried their hand at composition could hear and learn from the performance of their music. A small number of musicians had positions in the English Chapel Royal but the majority derived a livelihood through playing in the theatres, and through teaching—the more fortunate being attached to a noble household. Increasingly, however, there was work for players in the various kinds of orchestral concerts that came into being in the late seventeenth century.

The first series anywhere of regularly held concerts in one place, to which anyone irrespective of rank could be admitted as long as they paid as required, was initiated by John Banister in 1672. But even before this, what amounted to the same thing had been found in taverns that had a reputation for the musical entertainment they laid on. Customers paid for a drink or a meal and afterwards probably tipped the players, who, in the better ordered music-houses, sat by themselves at the end of the room. Whether all of them actually hired players to provide music or whether certain taverns were favoured by musicians who liked to meet, drink and entertain themselves and others through playing is not clear, but in his diary Samuel Pepys quite frequently alludes to having made music himself or listened to others at, for example, 'The Dolphin', 'The Cock', 'The Green Dragon', 'The King's Head', 'The Black Swan', 'The Blue Balls', 'The Dog' and other taverns in or around London. Such music-houses were not dependent on the custom of educated gentlemen like Pepys but were places of music for 'the common and ordinary sort of people', as Sir John Hawkins reports in his *History of the Science and Practice of Music* (1776).

15

Hawkins describes the most famous of the music-houses, 'The Mitre' at Wapping, taking his information from Ned Ward's *London Spy*.[1]

> . . . by the account which this author gives of it, the house, which was both a tavern and a music-house, was a very spacious and expensive building. He says that the music-room was a most stately apartment, and that no gilding, carving, painting, or good contrivance were wanting in the decoration of it; the seats, he says, were like the pews in a church, and the upper end being divided by a rail, appeared to him more like a chancel than a music-loft. Of the music he gives but a general account, saying only that it consisted of violins, hautboys, and[1] an organ. The house being a tavern, was accommodated as well to the purpose of drinking as music; it contained many costly rooms, with whimsical paintings on the wainscotting. . . . The owner of this house had, according to Ward's account, used every method in his power to invite guests to it; and, under certain circumstances, appeared to be not less solicitous for their safety than entertainment; for he had contrived a room under ground, in which persons were permitted to drink on Sundays, even during the time of divine service, and elude the search of the churchwardens.

Note what he says about having an organ there, a matter to which we will return in a moment.

Not all so-called music houses were taverns. Some were booths at fairgrounds in or around London. Music was also a useful diversion at the spas: Epsom and Tunbridge Wells, and Sadler's Wells in London, all of which were to be outstripped as fashionable watering-places of the bored and ailing aristocracy by Cheltenham and, above all, Bath. Coffee houses also competed as the venue for music meetings.

A Music Party, by Hogarth
(Fitzwilliam Museum;
Photo, Mansell Collection)

[1] *HH*, ii, 700.
[1] 'Hautboy' was one of the names given to the Baroque oboe: it is the same word differently spelt, and comes from the French 'haut-bois' = high wood.

Thomas Britton, the Musical Coalman, by J. Wollaston, 1703 (National Portrait Gallery)

The first advertisement for a public concert appeared in *The London Gazette* (no. 742) of 26 December 1672.

> These are to give notice, that at Mr *John Banisters* House (now called the Musick-School) over against the *George Tavern* in *White Fryers*, this present Monday, will be Musick performed by excellent Masters, beginning precisely at 4 of the clock in the afternoon, and every afternoon for the future, precisely at the same hour.

Banister continued to run his concerts at a number of music rooms until 1678, his last locale being in the Strand where presumably he might succeed in attracting a more fashionable clientele.[1] Other public music meetings of greater or lesser permanence were started about this time too. The most important was the series run by Thomas Britton the coalman, in the loft over his stable which he had converted for the purpose. From 1678 to his death in 1714 the weekly instrumental concerts, though his music room was 'not much bigger than the Bunghole of a Cask' (Ned Ward), seems to have attracted most of the best musicians in London, Handel included, as well as eminent members of the aristocracy. In fact, 'any Body that is willing to take a hearty sweat'. But there

[1] John Harley, *Music in Purcell's London* (London, Dennis Dobson, 1968), 135 *et seq*.

was a significant difference in the financial side of Banister and Britton's operations. Writing in about 1726 of music in public entertainments, a gentleman historian called Roger North informs us how Banister was paid:

> how and by what stepps Musick shot up to such request, as to croud out from the stage even comedy itself, and sit downe in her place and become of such mighty value and price as wee now know it to be, is worth inquiring after. The first attempt was low: a project of old Banister, who was a good violin, and theatricall composer. He opened an obscure room in a publik house in White fryars; filled it with tables and seats, and made a side box with curtaines for the musick. 1*s.* a peice, call for what you please, pay the reckoning, and *Welcome gentlemen.*[1]

North also says that Banister started his public concerts to raise money for himself. You see then, that far from playing set items on a programme, Banister's orchestra served as a kind of human juke-box, performing at a shilling a tune dances or any pieces they could manage with which their audience was familiar.

The habit, incidentally, of allowing the audience to 'call the tune' was to continue in the theatres into the early eighteenth century, as a means of keeping a restless audience quiet during the waiting period while the theatre was filling up before the performance started.

Returning to the difference between the way Thomas Britton and John Banister financed their concerts, Britton, finding he could not go on without charging admission even though he had the support of Sir Roger L'Estrange and other gentlemen in establishing his concerts, levied *an annual subscription* of ten shillings. Britton's circle included the leading players on hand, so he had no problem in selecting suitable soloists for the concertos which formed part of his repertoire—and the wide choice of music he had collected in parts, as shown in the catalogue of his effects sold after his death, testifies to a very comprehensive acquaintance with instrumental music of the late seventeenth and early eighteenth century. He had, in addition, a collection of fine musical instruments, including fourteen violins, and, at the end of an extensive and formidable list (for an apparently poor man who earned his living hawking coal around the streets of London on his back), 'A good harpsichord by Philip Jones. A Rucker's Virginal, thought to be the best in Europe', and 'An Organ of five stops, exactly consort pitch, fit for a room, and with some adornments may serve for any chapel, being a very good one.'[2]

Britton's subscription concerts, Hawkins writes, deserves our attention because

> it was the first meeting of the kind, and the undoubted parent of some of the most celebrated concerts in London.

It was the parent of the kind of concert which evolved throughout Europe on similar lines, and for which large-scale Baroque music in the form of the concerto was 'custom built'.

---

[1] *NOM*, 302–3.

[2] *HH*, ii, 793.

2.3 Some Definitions

It was during the seventeenth century that the major–minor system of tonality with which we are familiar today finally became general, and the traditional church modes[1] were largely dispensed with. That the *harmony* underlying every composition followed in a manner which was felt to be logical and correct according to the conventions of the time, was considered a matter of the first importance. To emphasize therefore the harmonic stability of the music, most Baroque compositions include a part called the **basso continuo** for instruments that could play the basic harmony as chords. Depending on what was available, this 'harmony part' was played by an organ, harpsichord, harp, lute, guitar or any such suitable instrument or instruments. Since each of these instruments has its own particular advantages and limitations, the continuo part was notated in such a way that the player could contribute to the ensemble *as his own instrument permitted*. Only the bass was given, and to it numerical figures and signs were added in accordance with an internationally known musical shorthand which indicated what harmonies should be added above the bass line. The bass itself was reinforced by whatever bass 'single-line' instruments were available— usually a cello or a viola da gamba. You can think for yourself which other instruments might also qualify for this role, and check your answer when you read the section that follows on the continuo. You might like to remember that the continuo is the section of the orchestra, or of the ensemble, which *continues* right through from beginning to end, playing the harmony in a fairly basic manner, against which we hear an embroidery of the same harmony in counter-point by the melody instruments concerned.

The **concerto** was the most popular Baroque form of orchestral music in the eighteenth century. You will be reading in units 7–9 about how closely related it was to the **sonata**, the form of instrumental music most commonly used for smaller ensembles. Essentially there is not much difference between them, apart from what naturally arises as a result of differences in scale, which have a bearing on the sound of the music as well as on its form. Incidentally, do not confuse these with Classical or Romantic concertos and sonatas which are generally longer piéces. The former are generally for a single soloist with orchestra and the latter may be for one instrument alone, as with the piano sonata, or for soloist with piano accompaniment.

In a Baroque sonata the number of melody instruments varies. It can be anything from one, in which case it is called a solo sonata, to five or six. The most popular form, however, was what we now call the trio sonata (perhaps illogically, because it doesn't have three but two melody instruments, but requires at least four players in performance). The instruments normally required to play a trio sonata would be two violins, cello, or viola da gamba, and harpsichord, organ or lute. Alternatively woodwind instruments might be involved. Sonatas vary also quite considerably as to their form and number of movements. In the mid-seventeenth century five was an average number; by the end of the Baroque era in the middle of the following century, sonatas of three and even two movements were being published. The leading figure in the development of the sonata was Arcangelo Corelli (1653–1713), whose influence few composers managed, or wished, to escape. The majority of Baroque sonatas are for violins, but sonatas were written for all the conventional melodic instruments of the period.

The melody instruments in a concerto are usually divided in a distinctive way, as you have already seen in the Corelli concerto grosso. The violins are divided

---

[1] For an explanation of 'mode' see *NDM*.

into firsts and seconds, violas may have an independent part or belong to the continuo section along with cellos, violas da gamba, harpsichord or organ and, if available, a violone or double bass. Apart from this division of the violins, however, in most concertos special melodic parts are written for one or more soloists. In a *solo concerto*, the single solo player is accompanied by, and plays with, the orchestra of strings and continuo. Wind instruments may infrequently be added. In a *concerto grosso* more than one soloist take a leading part; in fact there is a group of soloists which, however many players it comprises, is always called the *concertino*. The rest of the orchestra is called the *ripieno* or, alternatively, the *concerto grosso*. As you see, we have run into a confusion in terminology, with 'concerto grosso' being applied to both a kind of composition and a section of the orchestra involved in playing it.

A concerto is a piece in which instruments (and originally voices too) join literally in 'ensemble' music. By the late Baroque the term implies, besides simply the playing together, an element of struggle between groups in the whole orchestra: between the little ensemble of soloists, or concert*ino*, and the bigger ensemble, or concerto *grosso* (alias the ripieno). The size of the concertino could vary considerably as to the number of players and the instruments they played. By far the most popular line-up of soloists for a concerto grosso, nevertheless, was to have a concertino consisting of two violins and cello with harpsichord or organ. The ripieno or 'backing' might also have its own separate harpsichord or organ, making each group complete with its own keyboard-instrument continuo. When it did not, the same keyboard instrument served for both.

Concertos varied as to the number of movements into which they fell, but since the concerto's history is a good half century shorter than the history of the sonata and the influence of Vivaldi was strongly felt in its early days, the three-movement scheme so successfully demonstrated so often by Vivaldi was widely imitated.

Not surprisingly some composers did not have the same understanding of the terms as we do now, and initially the titles they gave their pieces might confuse us. There are very small-scale concertos, and very large-scale sonatas (the early Venetians particularly were fond of the latter), and there are concertos without a soloist or a distinct solo group at all. Such works are out of the general run of pieces written, however, and the most commonly used forms are those you find represented on the records: the solo sonata and the trio sonata, the solo concerto and the concerto grosso with a concertino consisting of two violins, cello and harpsichord or organ.

If you have spotted the fact that the most highly favoured choice of concertino was identical with that of the trio sonata group (two violins, cello and harpsichord or organ)—well done! This arrangement made it convenient for the four players of a trio sonata group to be able to play a concerto grosso if they wanted to. The backing would be missing of course, but this is seldom seriously missed since in the great majority of cases the ripieno only reinforces the solo parts when it joins in. Conversely, if the only music in parts which happened to be to hand were a trio sonata, this might well be 'scaled up' in performance by a large group of players, as long as they all used their discretion. The adaptability of Baroque music, and the down-to-earth practicality of the seventeenth- and eighteenth-century musician, is something on which we shall be commenting frequently.

We use the Italian terms for the little solo group, and for the group with which it is 'replenished'. (Italian *ri* = Latin and English *re-*; Italian *-pi-* = Latin and English *-pl-*. Compare *piano*. Latin *planus*, English *plain* = level or quiet.) And we use Italian for indicating the speed and character of movements. In the eighteenth century this was also the usual practice, except in France. The Italians were the creators and the natural leaders in the development of the sonata and the concerto, as also of violin playing to the close of the Baroque era.

The trio sonata did not in general present insuperable technical and interpretative hurdles to reasonably proficient players, and it had the characteristic property of sharing the melodic material between the two violins so that neither felt secondary to, or less important, than the other. For the technically interesting and adventurous, one turned to the solo sonata and solo concerto. Frequently these marked successive, competing stages in the technical development of rivalling virtuosos. The concerto grosso, on the other hand, was seldom blatantly exhibitionist in character, providing an attractive platform for the good player in its solo group while making only moderate demands on the weaker in its ripieno parts. It was a most considerate form—as amateur musicians quickly discovered. Hence the rapid spread of music clubs.

Let us consider examples of the forms introduced above, turning first to the trio sonata.

Exercise

Listen to the second movement Allegro from Corelli's op. 1 no. 1 trio sonata and decide, without reference to the score,

1 What instruments are involved?

2 How many beats there are in a bar?

3 How you would describe the melodic elements?

Play Baroque Music II side 1 band 1

Answers

1 Two violins, cello and harpsichord.

2 Four.

3 You should have mentioned the rising long-note theme of the opening, the quickly moving counterpoint, and commented on the extreme contrast between them. If you noticed that the rising-note theme is turned upside down in the middle and at the end, and becomes a descending line instead, well done.

Further Comment

Refer to the score in Unit 10.

In the score of this particular movement we have two parts written in the treble clef and two in the bass clef: the two violins, then the 'cello and harpsichord. Under the bottom stave you can see the numerals and signs of the musical shorthand I spoke about, from which the player 'realizes' or works out on his instrument an appropriately full version of the harmony indicated. I will keep the matter of who played the continuo, and how, for later, because it is an important aspect of Baroque music needing fuller discussion than I would wish to give it here. You might note, though, that the two bass parts are the same for most of the movement, and when they differ the upper of the two is most often fairly obviously a more ornamental version of the lower. (See bars 15, 24 and 33.)

The two violins are treated with complete equality, the second violin is by no means an alto to the first, it is above it in pitch as much as it is below. The compass within which they play is a moderate two-octaves-and-a-note up from middle C. Technically, none of the parts is difficult. The problem in performance lies in fitting the parts together in a coherent ensemble.

The rate at which the harmony changes is fairly constant. There is generally a change on every beat, and this is a characteristic of most Baroque music. As long as the 'harmonic rhythm', as the rate of change is called, is fairly slow we can accept any amount of melodic activity. The faster the harmonic rhythm, on the other hand, the more exciting the effect—until it becomes too fast to follow.

The purpose of the next exercise is to concentrate your attention on details in the melodic material used in this movement.

Exercise

Using the score as you listen this time, make a melodic analysis of the movement to indicate which instrument or instruments are playing element A, the rising long-note theme, and which B, the semiquavers. Look out for the inversions (when the rising figure descends) and label each of these as such.

Play Baroque Music II side 1 band 1

My Answer

bars 1–5	A violin 1, B violin 2
5–7	(going on to end of phrase on first beat of 9) A cello and harpsichord, B violin 1 with violin 2 joining in
9–13	A violin 2, B violin 1 and cello
13–14	Inversion: A violin 1, B violin 2
15–16	(going on to end of phrase first beat of 19) Inversion: A violin 2, B violin 1 and cello
19–20	(going on to first beat of 23) Inversion: A cello and harpsichord, B violins 1 and 2
23–24	Original version: A violin 1, B violin 2 and cello
25–26	(going on to first beat of 28) A cello and harpsichord, B violin 2 then violin 1
28–29	B continued interplay by violins
30–31	A violin 2
32–34	Inversion: A violin 2, B violin 1 and cello
35–38	Inversion: A cello and harpsichord, B violins

It is worth looking carefully to see these points in the score, and making sure that you are hearing them as you listen to the record. You should as a result of practice of this kind get better at selecting the 'information' you require from the score and from the music you listen to, and in this particular case you should appreciate the extreme economy of Corelli's composition.

Turn now to the *Concerto grosso op. 6 no. 8* 'The Christmas Concerto' by Corelli and look at the score. The instrumentation is given on the first page, making the affinity with the trio sonata clear. The top three staves bracketed together are the parts of the instruments we have been hearing in the trio sonata, two violins and cello. There are figures under the cello part, meaning that a harpsichord, organ or lute should fill in the harmonies. It is the continuo part of the solo group, or concertino. Underneath are arranged parts for violins 1 and 2, viola and 'Basso'. This last does not mean 'double bass', but is the continuo part of the ripieno, or accompanying players. The viola part is written on the alto clef, with middle C on the middle line. This is the most practical clef for the viola (except when required to play very high) because it encompasses the registers in which it usually plays—overlapping the upper part of the bass clef and the lower treble clef. You are advised to get accustomed to reading it because the alto clef will be confronting you whenever you open an orchestral score.

This arrangements of parts in the score is maintained throughout, and is helpful in isolating the concertino and ripieno sections.

Correction to Miniature Score

There is a mistake in bar numbering of the miniature score of Corelli *Concerto grosso op. 6 no. 8*, 'The Christmas Concerto', Edition Eulenburg, No. 348. Would you go through correcting the bar numbers? The second page was obviously missed out of the count and consequently the bar numbering from there onward is incorrect. What is marked as bar 20 on page 3 is bar 32 in fact. Please see to this. I shall be using the corrected bar numbering from now on.

The Baroque sonata and the concerto were closely related, and it is interesting to note that when Corelli's concertos were first published in England, by Walsh and Hare in 1715, they were given their Italian title and an additional English title which emphasizes this close relationship. It read: *XII Great Concertos or Sonatas, for two Violins and a Violincello [sic], or for two Violins more, a Tenor, and a Thorough-Bass which may be doubled at Pleasure.*

Exercise

To draw attention in an agreeable way to a connection between the solo sonata and the solo concerto, listen to a movement from each: the slow movement following the Allegro of Corelli op. 5 no. 1 (banded with the Allegro on Baroque Music II side 2 band 4) and a movement from Albinoni *concerto op. 9 no. 2* for oboe (Baroque Music III side 2 band 2). Do not refer to the scores.

1 Give the number of beats in a bar and describe the tempo of each movement.

2 How in each case does the composer encourage you to fix your attention on the solo instrument?

Play Baroque Music II side 2 band 4 and Baroque Music III side 2 band 2

My Comments

1 Both movements have three beats in a bar and are played at almost exactly the same slowish tempo.

2 The solo line in each case is distinct from its accompaniment rhythmically. It stands out by virtue of being placed higher in pitch than its accompaniment and different in timbre.

Further Discussion

There is more activity and less from phrase to phrase of the solo lines, but the accompaniments remain constantly rather unobtrusive throughout. In both there is a steady harmonic rhythm, and although in other Baroque slow movements composers make a feature of (particular) harmonic interest, it is not the case here where beauty of solo line has been the composers' main concern. Little imagination is required to hear the Corelli with an orchestral accompaniment or the Albinoni as a sonata for oboe and harpsichord.

The subscription concert or music club became such a common feature in English life during the early eighteenth century that scarcely a town was without one. The outcome, as Roger North writes, was that 'Musick shot up' in general popularity, and instruments makers, music teachers and publishers prospered. These music clubs were almost exclusively for the enjoyment of the members, who participated actively themselves. Ladies, and gentlemen on-lookers, were frequently excluded except on open nights: the accent was definitely on meeting *to play*—even alcoholic drinks being ruled out, when the members thought it more prudent.

Having decided to start a music club, the first requirement was to find a suitable room, then to equip it with chamber organ or a harpsichord. As we know, taverns proved very often to be the most convenient locales and some occasionally advertised the suitability of the accommodation they had. In *The Post Man*, 23 February 1717:

> To be Let. At the Two Golden Balls in Great Hartstreet Covent Garden, a very commodious Room with Galleries fit for the Entertainment of Dancing, but particularly for Consorts of Musick, approved of for that Use by the best Masters.

Other advertisements for this tavern's great room mention its suitability as a place for auctions of pictures, because of the 'advantageous Light newly made', and another adds that there were 'conveniences for Footmen without the Room'.[1]

The Pump Room, Bath an important concert hall.
(A. F. Kersting)

[1] Michael Tilmouth, *A Calendar of References to Music in Newspapers in London and the Provinces (1660–1719)*, (Royal Musical Association Research Chronicle no. 1, 1961), pp. 96 and 105.

You will remember that Thomas Britton had amongst his instruments a good harpsichord, a 'Rucker's Virginal, thought to be the best in Europe', and an organ of five stops. The more wealthy music clubs owned two keyboard instruments. Certainly, none would be able to function without one, and either a harpsichord or a small organ would have to be bought out of club subscriptions—or lent by one of the club's members. Britton's five-stop organ was of average size. Advertisements like these refer to larger instruments. *The Post Boy*, 3 January 1713:

> A Very good organ, with Eight entire Stops, and Four half Stops fit for any small Church, Chappel, or Hall to be sold: Enquire at Mr. John Cullen's.

and another:

> A Large House double organ [two manuals] with 11 Stops fit for a small Church or Chapple, is to be disposed of . . . enquire of Tho. Evans.[1]

A small chamber organ is almost as portable as a piano. It is approximately the same size as an upright piano except that it is taller and may be a little deeper from the keyboard to the back. It may be heavier, but it is more easily dismantled, of course. Buying an organ did not necessarily mean making costly structural alterations to the music room in order to house it. Today we tend to feel that wherever there is an organ, it is there to stay, but, at least during the whole of the eighteenth century, this was not of necessity the case. We may refer to John Marsh and his favourite instrument to give an interesting example of how at that time organs were *not* thought of as permanent fixtures. This solicitor with a passion for music,

> in 1783, removed . . . to his mansion-house of Nethersole, near Barham Downs, which he immediately furnished with a large organ, placing it between the entrance-hall and the dining parlour, with a front to each, and playable in both rooms.

Three years later he found it necessary to leave Nethersole, and bought a large house in Chichester,

> with a lofty and suitable room in it for his organ, and a good garden.[2]

Once the music room had been found and provided with a continuo instrument, a Gentlemen's Subscription Concert needed only to ensure that it had capable players to take the concertino parts in concertos, and it was ready for action. The concertino-ripieno structure of the concerto grosso was ideally suited to the small amateur orchestra. If members were not themselves good enough to take the leading parts, professional stiffening was hired, a practice which gave rise to the euphemistic differentiation between the man for whom music was a hobby and the one who played for a living. William Thomas Parke, a leading oboe player in London during the later eighteenth and early nineteenth century, draws the distinction in his amusing *Musical Memoirs*.[3]

[1] *The Post Man*, 1 March 1705.

[2] *Sainsbury's Dictionary of Musicians* (London, 1825), ii, 120.

[3] W. T. Parke *Musical Memoirs* (London 1830), i, 142.

It had been the custom for some years to distinguish amateur performers from professional, by giving the former the appellation of gentlemen players.

Such an expression strongly implied that the gentleman player wasn't any good, as Parke himself shows in an instance where a 'very indifferent' violinist is said to play 'in a very gentlemanly-like manner'.

If the good amateurs, or the professionals, took care of the continuo keyboard part and the solo parts, the club could function almost irrespective of how many other instrumentalists turned up, and what instruments they played. The essential parts were all there, anything in addition served to reinforce them and contribute weight in the tuttis. In the concerto grosso, contrast and relief was obtained not by alternating the solo players and the accompanists, but through taking off the ripieno, then adding them again to the concertino *which played all the time*. Thus, whenever the gentleman players joined in, they were led on the same parts by the professionals in the concertino. Because the concerto grosso was thus such a considerate form of orchestral composition, the amateur music scene was a flourishing one. And for the music publisher it was certainly a more important market than the court or the theatres where concertos were played. With the advent of the technically more difficult music in the *galant* style, from the 1750s and 60s, English music clubs came gradually to die out. But as an indication that there was still a market to be reckoned with in the late 'eighties, the title of a posthumous publication of music by Thomas Augustine Arne reads, *Six Favorite* [*sic*] *CONCERTOS for the Organ, Harpsichord, or Piano Forte with Instrumental Parts, for PUBLIC AND PRIVATE CONCERTS* (c. 1787).

2.5 Patronage

Professionals in the concertino may occasionally have been attached to the household of one of the music society's members, a fact one gathers from the dedicatory addresses introducing some publications of sonatas and concertos.

The private patron played an important and dominating role in the support of music-making during the Baroque era. As we have seen, orchestras were maintained throughout Europe, by musical heads of state—for the sake of form, or genuinely for their own enjoyment. If the head of state had a passion for opera, then the national budget could suffer as a result of the expenses incurred.

> The extravagant expenses of the court opera could only be covered if the patron received a steady revenue. In the budgets of German sovereigns who ruled a small country opera and ballet formed the largest single item of the expense account. The Duke of Brunswick, for one, relied not only on the most ingenious forms of direct and indirect taxation but resorted even to slave trade. He financed his operatic amusements by selling his subjects as soldiers so that his flourishing opera depended literally on the blood of the lower classes.[1]

It is not my intention here to investigate how the musical profession was maintained as a whole; it is a very large and fascinating subject. We are concerned with the particular importance of the patronage associated with the kinds of instrumental music which we shall be studying.

[1] *MBE*, 398.

As we have briefly considered, in the widest aspect patrons supported music by employing musicians. But a form of patronage which came strongly into its own during the Baroque era was that which was tied up with publication. In the seventeenth and eighteenth centuries, far more than at present, it was usual to circulate music in hand-copied parts because it was often cheaper to acquire a sonata or a concerto that way. But then as now, a certain prestige was attached to publication, and most composers of repute published some of their work. It meant that more people could play their music (although the size of an edition was generally very modest), and the composer also stood to gain financially. Since copyright laws were practically unknown and anyway were impossible to enforce, a composer had to ensure that he had a reasonable initial sum from the publication—knowing that if it proved to be a popular success it would quickly be pirated, over which editions he would have no control. The composer therefore normally came to an arrangement with a wealthy music lover whereby he received his patron's support in the form of preferment or money in return for a flattering dedication. As Roger North put it:[1]

> Nothing advanced musick more in this age than the patronage of the nobillity, and men of fortunes, for they became encouragers of it by great liberallitys, and countenance to the professors;

The style of the dedicatory address to a set of sonatas or concertos is conventionally flowery and lavish in its superlatives. But it might be that beneath the trimmings such an address is a useful reflection of its age. Take the first part of the following, for instance.

> Sir,
> Musick is so generally understood in this Age, and Honoured with the Patronage of the most Illustrious of both Sexes (many of whom are Excellent Judges & Curious Performers) that a Publisher cannot be too apprehensive of the Censure his Works may meet with, not only from the Professors of this Science, but also from Those by whose Approbation or Dislike he must Stand or Fall.
>
> It is a great Happiness to me, Sir, that the following Sonatas are Honoured with your Name, whose Skill, Ellegant Taste and Performance are Admirable. I presume not a Description of your Amiable Character, your Goodness & Condescention are apparent in permitting me to Subscribe my Self (which I do with the utmost Respect) Sir . . .
>
> (J. S. Humphries, *XII Sonatas op. 1*, 1734: to Henry Talbot, Esq.)

The composer is using 'publisher' in the literal sense of the one who has paid for the printing and upon whose authority it is issued—which meant the composer himself very often. Note the same meaning in the following dedication, as also the particular connotation of 'encourag'd (which you read in the comment by Roger North), and the information we get that the dedicatee could be helpful in recommending the music to his musical friends.

> S^r,
> Nothing but ye repeated instances I have rec^d of your Friendship & good Nature, cou'd have embolden'd me to prefix your Name to ye following Sonatas; As you have been pleas'd, when they were perform'd before you, to over look their faults, it has encourag'd me to publish 'em, not doubting

[1] *NOM*, 354.

but ye Approbation of a Gentleman of y^r nice Taste & Judgm^t in all ye politer Arts, will recommend 'em to ye Town, & hoping y^t their Author may obtain y^r Pardon, for y^s Presumption, on account of ye honour he has of being with ye greatest Esteem & respect

S^r

Your most Obliged
& most Obedient
humble Servant
William Corbett

(*Sonatas op. 4 libro 2°, c.* 1713: to Richard Edgcumbe, Esq.)

Never blind to the follies of the musical profession and the ludicrous conventions with which it was often encumbered, Benedetto Marcello 'sends up' the formal dedication in his widely read satire *Il teatro alla modo* ('The theatre à la mode') c. 1720.

> In dedicating his book to some great personage, [the modern poet] will try to find one rather rich than learned, and will make a bargain to reward some good mediator, say the cook or the major domo of the patron him-self, with a third of the proceeds of the dedication. From his patron he will ascertain in the first place the number and degree of the titles with which to adorn his name on the title page, augmenting the said titles by affixing 'etc., etc., etc., etc.' He will exalt the family and glories of his patron's ancestors, using frequently in his dedicatory epistle the terms 'liberality', 'generous soul', etc. and if (as sometimes happens) he finds in his personage no occasion for praise, he will say that he himself is silent in order not to offend the modesty of his patron, but that Fame with her hundred sonorous trumpets will sound his immortal name from pole to pole. Finally he will conclude by saying, in token of profoundest venera-tion, that he kisses the jumps of the fleas of His Excellency's dog.[1]

Patronage associated with publication in this form was an accepted fact of life in the seventeenth and eighteenth centuries, and to a lesser extent it continued later. We should be interpreting the matter wrongly if all such obsequious dedicatory addresses were written off as the despicable cringings of unprincipled musicians. One knows little of how agreements were reached between patron and composer, nor the degree of informality with which the terms might have been discussed, if at all. Vivaldi apparently got to know the Emperor Charles VI in 1728 in Trieste while the latter was in the thick of diplomatic activity which led to the Treaty of Seville (1729) and the Second Treaty of Vienna (1731). The music-loving Emperor, a performer himself who had even directed opera, was said to have spoken more with Vivaldi in two weeks than with his ministers in two years. It is highly improbable that a deal was ever spoken of but likely that Vivaldi *in gratitude* for a large sum of money, a gold medal and chain, and a knighthood, dedicated his twelve violin concertos op. 9 entitled *La Cetra* (1728) to the Emperor, not surprisingly mentioning in his dedicatory address his patron's 'magnanima protezzione' ('magnanimous protection').[2]

Johann Sebastian Bach was not so fortunate in his reward when he made the acquaintance of Frederick the Great at Berlin in 1747, at the court where one of his sons, Carl Philipp Emanuel, was harpsichordist. Having made a favour-

[1] *SRMH*, 520.

[2] *AV*, 17.

able impression on the King with his extemporizations on instruments in his collection of harpsichords and pianos, he is said to have requested the King, an accomplished flautist and amateur composer himself, for a theme of his own on which he might improvise—perhaps with the thought in mind of gaining some permanent mark of royal favour. Shortly afterwards he published his *Musical Offering*, a collection of contrapuntal pieces and a trio sonata based on the 'royal theme', dedicating it to the King,

> MOST GRACIOUS KING!
> In deepest humility I dedicate herewith to Your Majesty a musical offering, the noblest part of which derives from Your Majesty's Own August Hand. With awesome pleasure I still remember the very special Royal Grace when, some time ago, during my visit in Potsdam, Your Majesty's Self deigned to play to me a theme for a fugue upon the clavier, and at the same time charged me most graciously to carry it out in Your Majesty's Most August Presence. To obey Your Majesty's command was my most humble duty. I noticed very soon, however, that, for lack of necessary preparation, the execution of the task did not fare as well as such an excellent theme demanded. I resolved therefore and promptly pledged myself to work out this right Royal theme more fully and then make it known to the world. This resolve has now been carried out as well as possible, and it has none other than this irreproachable intent, to glorify, if only in a small point, the fame of a Monarch whose greatness and power, as in all the sciences of war and peace, so especially in music, everyone must admire and revere. I make bold to add this most humble request: may Your Majesty deign to dignify the present modest labor with a gracious acceptance, and continue to grant Your Majesty's Most August Royal Grace to
> Your Majesty's most humble and obedient servant,
> THE AUTHOR

Leipzig, July 7, 1747[1]

but the offering was accepted as the gift which, on the face of it, it apparently was, and the King did nothing concrete to 'continue to grant' his 'Most August Royal Grace' to the celebrated Kantor of St Thomas's, Leipzig.

You will be asked to analyse the Allegro movement from Bach's *Musical Offering* trio sonata later. It will help to make this more straightforward than it might be otherwise, if you can become familiar with it beforehand. To this end, begin now.

Play Baroque Music II side 1 band 4

Akin to the dedication, in that it brought the name of the person who chose this method of patronage into print, was the practice of subscribing to a musical publication. The list of subscribers for a work might show that it had become very much a society affair. The now completely forgotten English composer, Thomas Chilcot, organist of the Abbey at Bath, for example, obviously launched

[1] *BR*, 179.

his publications successfully in the fashionable circle in which he worked. For his *Twelve English Songs* (1744), sixty-five gentry and eighteen nobles were amongst the subscribers, while his *Six Concertos for the Harpsichord* (1756), attracted the support of twenty-four gentry and thirteen of the nobility, thirteen organists, and five of the clergy.

Exercise

Comment on the following address taken from the op. 7 concertos of Francesco Geminiani (1746), published in London and dedicated to perhaps the most exclusive of English music clubs, the Academy of Ancient Music. How does it differ from the dedications quoted earlier?

To the Academy of Ancient Music
GENTLEMEN,
A Dedication resulting purely from Regard and Affection, is perhaps as much a Rarity in England, as in other Countries. To the Disgrace of ARTS and SCIENCE, or at least, of their Professors, almost all Dedications from such, have in all Countries alike, arisen from the same Mercenary Motives.

From the Time of my first appearance in London, to this Hour, I have enjoy'd the Happiness of your Countenance and Favour, and such has been ever my sense of it, that I thought it highly deserving of my best Acknowledgments.

All men are fond of Praise, and perhaps it is to this Passion, that the most excellent Compositions of every kind have been principally owing; but all Praise hath not the same Effect: That of Ignorance operates on the Understanding, like jarring Dissonance upon the Ear, it shocks the sense it was address'd to please: whereas that of Discernment, like good Malody [*sic*] and perfect Harmony, at once fills and satisfies the whole Mind.

And here I cannot but observe, that as it hath been the peculiar Misfortune of the Science of MUSICK, that almost ev'ry Novice hath obtruded on the Publick his Crudities, which, however wretched, have nevertheless had their Advocates: So it ought to be the Consolation of every Professor who is desirous that Musick shou'd have its Standard as well as ev'ry other Science, that among You that Standard is not only held in the most religious Veneration, but is likely so to continue, as long as the Academy it Self shall last.

To please such Judges, and such only the following Peices were design'd in the composing of which great Study and Application hath been used, to make them acceptable to the Publick, but in particular to your Academy.[1]

My Comments

Geminiani was well aware of the 'payment or preferement for a flowering dedication' convention, but clearly has little sympathy with it from what we read here. Although he affects to despise it, however, the outcome of his own dedication would be an improvement in his standing with the Academy, which amounted to the same thing! As in the Humphries and Corbett dedications, as well as in the Bach, Geminiani compliments the skill and judgement of his dedicatees, but unlike them takes an unkind swipe at his rival composers in general. The dedication, incidentally, is to a society, the kind of compliment paid not infrequently by Italian composers to their academies.

[1] *TBC*, 273-4.

2.6 Taste

Corelli's outstanding merit, according to his pupil Geminiani, was not

> depth of learning . . . nor great fancy, or rich invention in melody or harmony; *but a nice ear and most delicate taste*, which led him to select the most pleasing harmonies and melodies, and to construct the parts so as to produce the most delightful effect upon the ear.[1]

(*My italics.*)

The cantatas of Bononcini were admired throughout the continent, 'for taste, expression, and grace', says Burney.[2] The English singer Anna Storace went to study in Italy, and 'acquired a very good taste, and first gave us *l'avant goût* of Marchesi's embellishments'.[3] L. A. Koželuh of Vienna's compositions were, 'in general excellent, abounding with solidity, good taste, correct harmony'.[4] In fact, despite Hawkins's objection that it was 'a cant phrase much in use with the musical connoisseurs',[5] you will find that practically every single description of a musical performance, and every account of the merits possessed by a composer or an instrumentalist, written in the eighteenth century, includes a reference to *taste*.

Taste was musical etiquette.

In general 'taste' might refer to the capacity of the composer or the instrumentalist to observe the convention, by doing what was appreciated. What satisfied the public taste of a nation at any time was the music fashionably acceptable to the audiences which listened to it—irrespective of whether it was in a style which exhibited a particular degree or aesthetic refinement.

Some writers used the word in a deliberate, confined sense, implying that taste had something to do with the emotional significance given to the music, that it was the quality which made the music seem relevant to the listener.

As Leopold Mozart—Wolfgang Amadeus Mozart's father—succinctly expressed it:

> Everything turns on good performance—everyday experience confirms this rule. Many a half-composer is pleased and delighted when he hears his musical Galimathias performed by good players who know how to apply the passion, which he had not even thought about, in its proper place, how to make the greatest possible distinction in the characters, which has never occurred to him, and consequently how, by means of a good delivery, to render the whole wretched scribble tolerable to the ears of the listeners.

But, he goes on to say,

> The good delivery of a composition in the present taste is not as simple as those people believe who think they are doing very well if, following their own ideas, they ornament and contort a piece in a truly idiotic fashion and who have no conception whatever of the passion that is supposed to be expressed in it.[6]

---

[1] *BH*, ii, 442. [2] *Id.*, 636. [3] *Id.*, 900.

[4] *Id.*, 960. [5] *HH*, ii, 903.

[6] From Leopold Mozart's violin method (1756), chapter 12; see *SRMH*, 599–600.

Wolfgang and Leopold Mozart (Royal College of Music)

The Italian theorist, Giorgio Antoniotto[1] held that music should be written 'with taste and judgement'. And in William Waring's translation of Rousseau's dictionary of music (*The Complete Dictionary of Music*, 1776) in the article on *Taste*, we find this astute view put forward:

> It seems that taste is more particularly connected with the smaller expression, and sensibility to the greater.

Geminiani's explanation of taste is directed towards the performer:

> What is common call'd good Taste in singing and playing, has been thought for some Years to destroy the true Melody, and the Intention of their Composers. It is supposed by many that a real good Taste cannot possibly be acquired by any Rules of Art; it being a peculiar Gift of Nature, indulged only by those who have naturally a good Ear: And as most flatter themselves to have this Perfection, hence it happens that he who sings or plays, thinks of nothing so much as to make continually some favorite Passages or Graces, believing that by this Means he shall be thought to be a good Performer, not perceiving that playing in good Taste doth not consist of frequent Passages, but in expressing with Strength and Delicacy the Intention of the Composer. This Expression is what every one should endeavour to acquire, and it may be easily obtained by any Person, who is not too fond of his own Opinion, and doth not obstinately resist the Force of true Evidence.

[1] Giorgio Antoniotto, *L'Arte Armonica* (London, 1760), 92.

32

Exercise

In this exceptional passage,[1] Geminiani says not only what good taste is, but goes further in an attempt to clarify his definition by saying also what he considered to be in bad taste.

What is he really saying?

My Comment

The drift of his argument seems to me to fall into two parts: (i) you should let the music speak for itself, exactly as the composer meant it to be, not distorted by unintended and inappropriate extemporary decoration; and (ii) good taste is equated with suitable expression and sensibility. Both points you will notice in the passages quoted from Leopold Mozart too.

Discussion

The first point may strike you as unexpected, because performance practices have changed a great deal since the Baroque era, and we are now very much 'note-bound' compared with then. Unless we are consciously trying to get back into the style, we do not usually play what is *not* written. At that time, however, the musician probably would do this—as you will see shortly, when we look at the matter of extemporary additions in a performance. Of course, by 'note-bound', I am referring to the professional orchestral player and the concert soloist today, not the player of folk music, and the jazz or pop musician.

Good taste, then, consists in expressing with strength or delicacy the composer's intention—say Geminiani and Leopold Mozart. It is not, therefore, essential for a performer to have a voice of superlative quality, or a brilliant instrumental technique, as long as what he has is adequate to convey the character or the emotional content with which the music he performs has been invested. In the Baroque period the outstanding example of what could be achieved by good taste alone must surely be that of Handel's performance as a singer: Hawkins relates that

> without a voice (Handel) was an excellent singer of such music as required more of the pathos of melody than a quick and voluble expression . . . he once gave proof that a fine voice is not the principal requisite in vocal performance. . . . At a concert at the house of Lady Rich he was prevailed on to sing a slow song, which he did in such a manner, that Farinelli, who was present, could hardly be persuaded to sing after him.[2]

His prowess as a string player also leaned heavily on his musicianship instead of on a sure technical grounding.

> He had never been a master of the violin, and had discontinued the practice of it from the time he took to the harpsichord at Hamburg; yet, whenever he had a mind to try the effect of any of his compositions for that instrument, his manner of touching it was such as the ablest masters would have been glad to imitate.

[1] F. Geminiani, *An Introduction to a good taste in Music*, 2.

[2] *HH*, ii, 913. Farinelli was the leading *castrato* singer in Europe at the time. He was able to command astronomical fees for appearances in opera.

In the early eighteenth century a valuable lead on what the French regarded as constituting good taste in music is given in the *Traité du bon goût en musique* (1705) by Jean Laurent le Cerf de La Viéville, Lord of Freneuse. Presenting his views in the form of a conversation between educated people of noble birth, he puts his own forward in the person of a Chevalier, who suggests,

> 'There are two great ways of knowing good and bad things: by our inward feeling and by the rules. We know the good and the bad only by these means. What we see and what we hear pleases us or displeases us. If one listens only to the inward feeling, one will say, "It seems to me that that is good, or that it is not." On the other hand, the masters, the skilled, following the observations they have made, have established precepts in every craft..These comprised whatever had seemed to them to be the best and the surest. The established precepts are the rules, and if one consults them regarding what one sees and what one hears, one will say that this is good or is not good, according to such and such a rule, or for such and such a reason. These masters were men; were they incapable of being deceived? The authority of the rules is considerable, but after all it is not a law. Inward feeling is still less sure, because each should distrust his own, should distrust that it is what it should be. Who will dare flatter himself that he has a fortunate nature, endowed with sure and clear ideas of the good, the beautiful, the true? We have all brought into the world the foundation of these ideas, more or less clear and certain, but since our birth we have received, and this it is sad and painful to correct, a thousand false impressions, a thousand dangerous prejudices, which have weakened and stifled within us the voice of uncorrupted nature.

> 'I think that in this uncertainty and confusion the remedy is to lend to the inward feeling the support of the rules, that our policy should be to correct and strengthen the one by the other, and that it is this union of the rules and the feeling which forms good taste. To listen attentively to the inward feeling, to disentangle it, and then to purify it by the application of the rules; there is the art of judging with certainty, and therefore I am persuaded that good taste is the most natural feeling, corrected or confirmed by the best rules.'[1]

In the last lines we have the crux of the matter: of course the received opinions about what is felt to be acceptably 'natural' in feeling and expression is constantly being updated. And the conventions regarding acceptable practices in composition, the 'rules' of music, have never been regarded as inviolable by the greatest masters. One had to learn what there was to learn, said Handel, then go one's own way. The popularly held likes and dislikes in one country, moreover, are seldom the same ones as one finds in another, and in the Baroque era there was a distinct difference between the commonly held views of Italian and French musicians. Frederick the Great's flute teacher, J. J. Quantz, observes in the famous flute tutor-book he published in 1752:

> [The Italians and French] have been seduced, as it were, into setting themselves up as arbiters of good taste in music, and, since for some time past no foreigner has objected, for several centuries they have actually been, so to speak, the musical lawgivers. From them, good taste in music was brought afterwards to other people.[2]

[1] *SRMH*, 491–2.

[2] *Id.*, 592.

So violently hostile were the Italian and the French views felt to be, that a literary battle with the combatants led by two Frenchmen, the Lord of Freneuse (for the French) and the Abbé François Raguenet (for the Italian) became the focus of a great deal of public interest in France during the first twenty years or so of the eighteenth century. In England public taste in the eighteenth century was heavily indebted to the lead given by the many Italians resident in the country; while Germany, strongly influenced by aspects of both French and Italian music, was by the end of the Baroque era cultivating a 'mixed taste', as Quantz called it.

To sum up: according to the context, taste could mean sensibility, skill, or a code of good manners in music conventionally accepted by society. The most sincere attempt to define the term, by an eighteenth-century writer, was published in Waring's *The Complete Dictionary of Music* (1776). It sums up very neatly what the other authors quoted earlier had been saying, but does so in a style which surpasses them all in poetic beauty:

> Of all natural gifts, taste is that which is most felt and least explained; It would not be what it is, if it could be defined: for it judges of objects, in which the judgement is not concerned, and serves, as it were, as Spectacles to reason.

> Each man has his peculiar taste, by the which he gives to things, which he calls beautiful and excellent, an order which belongs to himself alone. One is touch'd with pathetic pieces; the other prefers a gay air.

> Genuis creates, but taste makes the choice; and a too abundant genius is often in want of a severe censor, to prevent it from abusing its valuable riches. We can do great things without taste, but it is that alone which renders them interesting. It is taste, which makes the composer catch the ideas of the poet: It is taste, which makes the executant catch the ideas of the composer.

> It is taste, which furnishes to each whatever may adorn and augment their subject; and it is taste, which gives the audience the sentiments of their agreements.

In a study of Baroque music one must be aware of how essential musicians felt it to be to observe the general tenets of good taste held by the society in which they worked. I have emphasized in this introduction to the matter *the concern for taste* musicians had in the seventeenth and eighteenth centuries. We will be observing in the music details of compositions written in good taste. But in trying to appreciate and evaluate this music, and in trying to re-create it in performance, we are faced with a serious problem. Taste in all aspects of music has changed so much since many of the pieces we shall be looking at were first performed over three hundred years ago, that it may be argued that no present-day performance will sound as the composer probably imagined it should, or as it would originally have been played.

Back in the late eighteenth century Burney was aware of the difficulties involved in the interpretation of music from a past age. He writes about the sixteenth-century music of the Netherlands school:

> There is, indeed, as little chance for a musician of the present age to perform such productions in the manner of the times in which they were composed, as to pronounce a foreign language as well as his own; and if, against all calculation, he should succeed, this Music will still be an unknown tongue to the public.[1]

---

[1] *BH*, ii, 259.

Not only have all the instruments been developed technically, with resultant changes in tone colour, volume, and the usual means of articulation, but, partly as a result of these developments, partly as the outcome of the natural evolution of playing technique, we have arrived at a situation in which the music is performed differently as well. But this—Baroque music made to conform to current taste—is what we are used to, and comparatively few people are perturbed that it only faintly resembles what we know from the benefit of modern scholarship to have been its former character. It would seem reasonable to expect performers to study the music in the context of its period and as far as possible to present it in a manner which would be in accordance with the standpoint of the composer. But this is often a vain hope, and eighteenth-century music is all too frequently played in an anachronistic way. A piano might, for example, be used instead of a harpsichord or organ for the continuo. Or, although rarely perhaps by now, the keyboard continuo instrument may be dispensed with in a modern performance of a concerto, thus depriving the ensemble of its foundation, and misrepresenting the balance of sonorities which the composer had imagined. When this occurs, it shows that the conductor has overlooked the essential character of Baroque music, failing to realize that the main feature which distinguishes it from the music of any other style is precisely the one he chose to neglect, the continuo which was at the basis of the Baroque concept of harmony.

No introduction to the subject of taste in early eighteenth-century music would be complete without a word on French and Italian views. Although musicians of these nations may not, as Quantz says, deliberately have set themselves up as the arbiters of good taste in music, they undoubtedly exerted the strongest influence on the composition and performance of Baroque music. Their tastes are shown in the kind of compositions they fostered.

Exercise

You have on record the overture to Lully *Le Divertissement de Chambord*, a pair of Rigaudons from Boismortier *Petites Sonates op. 66 No. 4* and Rameau *Pièces de clavecin (1741)* 'La Livri', from which you may judge what elements were appreciated in the French style. There is a greater choice of Italian music on record. Take, for example, the Corelli op. 5 solo sonata, and the concerto movements by Vivaldi and Albinoni.

Listen to these movements and decide how they differ. What kind of pieces are they? Consider the choice of melodic material and the texture of these pieces of music.

My Answer

We cannot make a strict comparison because the kinds of pieces are different— but this, of course, is a reflection on French and Italian taste. Whereas the French preferred to write refined suites of dances for court and theatre, the Italians concentrated on larger-scale forms of instrumental music, the sonata and concerto. The quality I feel to be strongly evident in the Corelli solo sonata Allegro and in the Vivaldi is confidence, boldness. Both are concerned with simple melodic material; scales in the opening of the Vivaldi, arpeggios in the Corelli. Both are incisive in style; the one a concerto, the other a sonata. The Lully overture opens a suite of dances. The Boismortier duet consists of short movements, again mostly dances. The Rameau is simply called a 'piece' for harpsichord with violin and viola da gamba. The Lully and Rameau are distinguished by their rich texture.

Further Comment

As the leading French proponent for the Italian style, Abbé François Raguenet wrote (1702), the French play with great refinement and gentle delicacy, they 'flatter, tickle, and court the ear'.[1] The texture and instrumental colour of French music may be richer than much Italian music, but the zestful style of Italian writing (and playing) the confident themes, surprising modulations and contrapuntal skill make it a more exciting style than the French. Raguenet:

> It is not to be wondered that the Italians think our music dull and stupefying, that according to their taste it appears flat and insipid, if we consider the nature of the French airs compared to those of the Italian.

If we consider the melody of 'La Livri' by Rameau, we find it has a plaintive quality, and there is a tendency with each phrase to sink so that it ends lower than it begins. The opening phrase begins with a leap from g' to c'' but it ends on d', for example. Comparing this movement with the less impassioned of the Italian slow movements, that of the Corelli op. 5 solo sonata, it is softer and less expansive, but this, perhaps, is the quality one admires or finds satisfying. It is ordered and predictable; the Boismortier duet is similarly uncomplicated and predictable, embellished with delicate trills and appoggiaturas.

It is probably more difficult to appreciate the distinctive qualities of French Baroque music than those of the Italian. We live at a time of innovation and progress, and naturally respond with admiration to the adventurous and striking —qualities we recognize in music of the Italian style. But we are also approaching Baroque music at a disadvantage; being used to the overwhelming noise of much 'pop' music, and the instrumental colours and harmonic excitement of Romantic music. In comparison, the exquisite refinement and poise of much French music may unsympathetically be considered uneventful and dull.

In the course of the next few weeks you have an opportunity to become accustomed to Baroque music in the French, Italian, and mixed styles. See if you can clarify your thoughts by listening to these pieces again. You will get far more from the immediacy of listening than from reading about the distinctions.

2.7   Extemporary Embellishment

The greatest single obstacle to be overcome in presenting eighteenth-century music is that of extemporary embellishment. It is possible to direct an eighteenth-century sized orchestra (with the characteristic balance of wood-wind and strings) to play with the correct type of articulation, but the result would still be wanting in authenticity unless the soloists and members of the continuo section had learnt the art of ornamentation, and could apply embellishments appropriately in performance. So far, in recent times, this art falls outside the normal training in instrumental music, and not all players have the opportunity later on to study it. Besides, it is one which is more easily learned from a teacher than from a book, and few teachers who know the eighteenth-century style of playing are available when required. One author, William Turner, went so far as to write in his *Sound Anatomiz'd in a Philosophical Essay on Musick* (1724):

---

[1] *SRMH*, 477.

As to *Shakes*, *Beats*, *Back-falls* etc. which some Authors have treated of, I find it to no Manner of Purpose to give any Account of them, for to those who cannot take them by *Nature*, all *Human Art* is lost, and all other Things in this *Science* will prove ineffectual.

But other writers do 'give an Account' of the ornaments, of course, and the accepted method of playing them, if not the complete style of their presentation, may be learned from a book, as you will see shortly.

You have already heard some of Geminiani and Leopold Mozart's comments to the soloist who embellished his part inappropriately. The over-use of embellishments, but particularly by ripieno players, was criticized very strongly by many other writers in the eighteenth century too. Robert Bremner, a leading Scottish publisher based in London, in *Some Thoughts on the Performance of Concert Music* (1770), addressed his remarks to the Gentlemen of the ripieno. It is clear from his tone that these players were accustomed to indulging far too much in inappropriate ornamentation. Bremner reminds them that they were not, after all, soloists, and were *not* at liberty to introduce graces as and when they pleased.[1]

> As gentlemen performers are, in general, fond of applying the graces of the finger, we shall consider them further in shewing the difference between solo and concert playing; a distinction so necessary to be made, that without it every performer in concert must be in danger of mis-applying his abilities.
>
> A solo-player being the principal entertainer during his performance . . . all the different graces of the bow and finger may be applied by him, when and where he pleases. . . .
>
> The concert, or orchestra player, on the contrary, is only a member of that whole by which a united effect is to be produced; and if there be more than one to a part, he becomes no more than a part of a part; therefore his performance, with that of those who play the same part, must, like the unisons of an organ or harpsichord, coincide so as to pass for one entire sound, whether loud or soft. Should any one from the leader down-ward deviate in the least from this uniformity, it may easily be supposed that his performance must, for that time, be worse than nothing. . . .
>
> From what has been observed above, it must follow, that when gentlemen are performing in concert, should they, instead of considering themselves as relative parts of one great whole, assume each of them the discretional power of applying tremolos, shakes, beats, appogiaturas, together with some of them slurring, while others are articulating, the same notes; or, in other words, carrying all their different solo-playing powers into an orchestra performance; a concert thus rebellious cannot be productive of any noble effect.

Precisely on account of the unsatisfactory outcome to the kind of rebelliousness described by Bremner, embellishment by professional orchestral players is thought to have been rare. The best orchestral directors, like Lully and Corelli, who were renowned for the neatness of their ensemble playing and unanimity of bowing, would not tolerate it. The soloist was less likely to upset a performance by over-embellishing his part than a ripieno player was, but he could

[1] R. Bremner, *Some Thoughts on the Performance of Concert Music*, pp. ii–iii. This valuable little monograph is hidden away in one of the author's commercial publications, J. G. C. Schetkey, *Six Quartettes op. 6* (London, 1777).

harm his reputation all the same if he offended badly against the accepted tenets of good taste. Of course, he was *expected* to introduce a certain amount of free embellishment. However, he should not assume that the part which he improvised would necessarily be an improvement on the printed copy, and should not therefore avoid playing what was provided for him simply to prove his capabilities.

> But whatever Latitude may be allowed the Performer for embellishing these Pieces with any additional Taste of his own, it is presumed he will punctually attend to the essential Harmony of the Bass, where every Passage ought to be taken in its very *identical Notation*, because some good Effect is generally aimed at: And therefore it may reasonably be supposed, that those Contrivances, which have been the Result of Time and Thought, are not very likely to be improved by any Performance *extempore*.[1]

The advice offered to instrumentalists of the ripieno is addressed, you might note, to 'gentlemen players', whereas the author of these last remarks does not have the offending gentlemen particularly in mind.

But, now that we know it was an important, characteristic feature of Baroque music, what do we mean by 'appropriate extemporary embellishment'?

At its most basic it had to do with the use of musical ornaments, then in a wider sense with the improvisation of additional notes to (or around) the given part.

Towards the end of the seventeenth century, French lutenists and harpsichord players had brought a measure of rationalization to the earlier practice of either writing out in full or using a wide range of personal signs to indicate ornaments in music, by standardizing the names and signs used. Theorists felt the importance of ornaments to varying degrees. While some compared musical ornaments, or *Agréments*, to the decoration on buildings, agreeable but not essential, others saw them as vital, like the spices in cooking without which the food is flat and insipid. The French and Italian differences in taste are seen clearly in their attitude to ornamentation.[2] In France (particularly in keyboard music, though less in music for strings) the improvised ornament tended to fall out of use by the end of the seventeenth century in favour of the ornament specifically indicated. However, Italian composers preferred not to conventionalize so much and to leave the choice of ornament to the discrimination of the solo player. They knew that although they were not normally written out, it was usual for players to improvise additions to the given notes, in slow movements especially, and to put in trills on the penultimate melodic note of a cadence. As a result largely of Lully's discipline, French players became expert at playing the specific ornaments indicated in the dance music they performed. They were not permitted to indulge in improvising on their parts, as the Italians did, and they were expected from their knowledge of the style and execution of all the ornaments to be able to play the appropriate one in cases where the composer had simply indicated with a little cross above the note that an embellishment of some kind was to be added there (the more common Italian practice).

If you turn to the scores of the movements by Rameau and Boismortier in unit 10 you will see this kind of indication (+).

---

[1] Charles Avison, *Six Sonatas for the Harpsichord with Accompanyments for Two Violins and Violoncello*, Op. 5: last paragraph of 'Advertisement'.

[2] *HVP*, 285.

As taste changed, the favourite ornaments did too, and the kind of embellishment and style of improvised addition was not allowed to get too firmly fixed in tradition. Although some of the same symbols remained, their meaning varied—another obstacle to present-day interpretation of Baroque music. We need not pursue the study of ornamentation here, having emphasized that in the seventeenth- and eighteenth-century music which we are considering it was an indispensable feature. As an indication of the range of ornaments used, here are two articles from Francesco Geminiani's *The Art of Playing the Violin* (1751), the first tutorbook aimed at the professional.

Example 18 contains

all the ornaments of expression, necessary to the playing in a good taste . . . certain rules of art are necessary for a moderate genius, and may improve and perfect a good one. To the end therefore that those who are lovers of music may with more ease and certainty arrive at perfection, I recommend the study and practice of the following ornaments of expression, which are fourteen in number; namely,

1st a plain shake (⋔) 2nd a turned shake (⤺) 3rd a superior apogiatura (♪) 4th an inferior apogiatura (♪) 5th holding the note (–) 6th staccato (|) 7th swelling the sound (◢) 8th diminishing the sound (◣) 9th piano (p.) 10th forte (f.) 11th th. anticipation (♪) 12th separation (♪) 13th a beat (//) 14th a close shake (⌇) From the following explanation we may comprehend the nature of each element in particular.

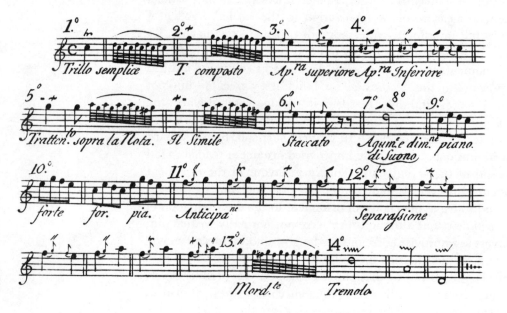

Example 19

In this is shown how a single note (in slow time) may be executed with different ornaments of expressions.

You might be astonished to see the last ornament listed: the close shake or tremolo as Geminiani calls it. We'd say vibrato. In modern string playing vibrato is used **all** the time, and in wind playing too it has come to be fashionable since the Second World War.

When a player applies a vibrato the pitch of the note is raised and lowered slightly to a regular pulse. The amount by which it varies and the frequency or speed of the pulse affect the tone-quality. In effect the note is enriched; the possibly rather dead-sounding, 'straight' note may be given a quality of warmth or excitement, for example, when given a 'close shake'. The following is also taken from Geminiani's tutorbook, in which account you will notice at the end of the first paragraph he recommends using vibrato as often as is practical, which means all the time except in fast passages.

Of the Close Shake

This cannot possibly be described by notes as in former examples. To perform it, you must press the finger strongly upon the string of the instrument, and move the wrist in and out slowly and equally, when it is long continued swelling the sound by degrees, drawing the bow nearer to the bridge, and ending it very strong it may express majesty, dignity, etc. But making it shorter, lower and softer, it may denote affliction, fear, etc. and when it is made on short notes, it only contributes to make their sound more agreeable and for this reason it should be made use of as often as possible.

Men of purblind understandings, and half ideas may perhaps ask, is it possible to give meaning and expression to wood and wire; or to bestow upon them the power of raising and soothing the passions of rational beings? But whenever I hear such a question put, whether for the sake of information, or to convey ridicule, I shall make no difficulty to answer in the affirmative, and without searching over-deeply into the cause, shall think it sufficient to appeal to the effect. Even in common speech a difference of tone gives the same word a different meaning. And with regard to musical performances, experience has shown that the imagination of the hearer is in general so much at the disposal of the master, that by the help of variations, movements, intervals and modulation he may almost stamp what impression on the mind he pleases.

These extraordinary emotions are indeed most easily excited when accompanied with words; and I would besides advise, as well the composer as the performer, who is ambitious to inspire his audience, to be first inspired himself; which he cannot fail to be if he chooses a work of genius, if he makes himself thoroughly acquainted with all its beauties; and if while his imagination is warm and glowing he pours the same exalted spirit into his own performance.

Another great virtuoso, Giuseppe Tartini (1692–1770), who was very influential as a violin teacher through the 'School of Nations' he founded and ran at Padua, took a different stand. He held that vibrato should be treated like any other detail of ornamentation and applied only at the appropriate points—long notes on which the vibrato could be played deliberately (slower than is usual today), and in time with the subdivision of the beat of the movement. He was supported by Leopold Mozart, who derided the players 'who tremble consistently on each note as if they had the palsy'.[1]

On long notes it was customary to apply the *messa di voce*, a billowing effect obtained by beginning the note very softly, increasing the tone as the middle of the bow was reached then diminishing to end softly. While Tartini instructs the player to produce the effect *by varying the pressure of the bow*, Geminiani allows vibrato also to contribute to the 'swelling' of the note—which is a more natural way of doing so, and in keeping with the vocal practice of the time too.

But apart from ornaments—and the French and Italians differed a lot in their feeling for ornamentation—the art of embellishment extended to adding notes to the part that was given. Players regarded the printed notes of a slow movement (particularly) as only the skeleton on which they had to put the flesh, hence the importance to the character of the performance of how appropriately they added their 'passages' or 'divisions'. The examples of such additions which have come down to us show that these were often sensitively improvised to heighten the natural points of tension and relaxation in the melody, which substantiates the statement made in 1753 by Carl Philipp Emanuel Bach, in his *Essay on the true art of playing keyboard instruments*: 'Embellishments provide opportunities for fine performance as well as much of its subject matter. . . . Without them the best melody is empty and ineffective.'[2]

To give an idea of ornamentation *through looking*, rather than listening, here are two versions by Handel of an air for harpsichord. The one, from the third suite for harpsichord, is ornamented quite explicitly, with the most significant notes of the melody printed in Handel's own edition of 1720 in large noteheads. The other, an earlier version of the same piece, is clean of all additions.

[1] *HVP*, 387.

[2] C. P. E. Bach *Essay on the true art of playing keyboard instruments*, trans. and ed. William J. Mitchell (London, Cassell, 1949), p. 79.

Exercise

Listen carefully now to the slow movement of Corelli's op. 5 solo sonata. The embellishments which are included in the recording on Baroque Music II are not printed in the violin part given here. This is the part as it was originally published, the skeleton melody around which the performer wove his own interpretation. Follow this part and decide:

1 What is the nature of the embellishment you hear on record; the application of ornaments to important notes in the phrase, the addition of scalic passages or both?

2 Where in the movement is the embellishment most profuse? Give the bar numbers.

3 Are there, in fact, any bars which are not embellished at all?

'4 There is a musical sequence at bars 15–17; the same melody and harmonic progression is written three times consecutively, a step higher up the scale with each repetition. What do you notice about the embellishment here?

43

5 Make a general comment on the use of embellishment in this movement. Presumably, it must be felt to contribute to the beauty of the line, or it would not be there, but how does it do this?

Play Baroque Music II side 2 band 4

My Answer

1 Both, although the additional scalic runs are more obvious.

2 Bars 18, 40 and 41.

3 Yes, bars 5, 9–10, 21, 26–7, 35, 39.

4 The embellishments are also the same, heightening thus the satisfaction one feels on following a well-managed sequence.

5 C. P. E. Bach's comment about the best melody being empty and ineffective without embellishments is most apt here. The running passages lead the ear on to the important structural points of the melody. These are almost invariably on the accented first beat of the bar, and are played their full length. The scalic passages follow the contour of the 'skeleton melody notes' on unstressed beats. The added passages soften the angularity of the bare melodic line. The ornaments on particular notes add variety in colour (the sound of a trilled note having a different 'colour' from the straight note), and from their conventional usage, draw attention to cadence points. The embellishments contribute grace through their 'softening' influence on the melodic line, while yet adding excitement, passion, through the controlled weight of additional notes.

Further Comment

The score of the movement as you have heard it played is in unit 10. Refer to this now.

The embellished violin part is printed on the uppermost of the three staves; under it is the bare skeleton, which you will recognize, and the continuo part is indicated by the figured bass line.

Listen to the Adagio again, following the score, and noting in particular how, for example, the line is 'softened' in bars 14–15, while yet, to heighten the climax of the phrase in bars 18–19, the embellished line departs from the 'official' line which moves by step, and introduces an expressive leap of a seventh (from d''' to e'').

Play Baroque Music 2 side 2 band 4

The passages are, in fact, a record of the manner in which Corelli himself apparently played the movement.

So very highly was the taste of this musician regarded in the early eighteenth century that editions were issued in Amsterdam and London in about 1710 and 1711, having 'yᵉ graces to all yᵉ adagios . . . where the author thought proper', as the London version puts it. By issuing thus an 'official' account of Corelli's embellishments, the publishers were doing the equivalent of issuing the definitive performance of a piece recorded by a modern composer or his finest interpreter.

You may be in a position to note something interesting for yourself if you happen to live near a record library which stocks the old 78 rpm recordings of the 1930s. If you should compare the style of playing then with what we customarily hear today you are likely to realize that, leaving aside the quality of the early recordings, the actual sound of a solo violin or of a symphony orchestra has changed. There has been a marked change of taste in a matter of forty years, which has its effect primarily on tempo, vibrato and the style of joining up the notes of a melody. Whereas now we regard it as rather important to maintain a fairly constant tempo throughout a movement unless the composer indicates a change, early recordings remind us that it is not so long ago that the tempo direction 'Allegro' might encompass a liberal variation, the music naturally becoming faster as things got exciting then slackening considerably in impetus as they quietened down. Most wind players and even some string players refrained from using vibrato, but it is noticeable that string players were in the habit of *sliding* from note to note in expressive music, particularly up to the important notes in a melody. This use of *portamento* is generally thought distasteful now, if not decidedly vulgar.[1] Geminiani worked out a system of fingering in order to avoid shifting the hand while a finger slid up or down the string; nevertheless *portamento* was obviously a feature of the style of some great players at that time, as Burney reflected at the end of the century.

> Geminiani, however, was certainly mistaken in laying it down as a rule that 'no two notes on the same string, in shifting, should be played with the same finger'; as beautiful expressions and effects are produced by great players in shifting, suddenly, from a low note to a high, with the same finger on the same string.[2]

The art of embellishment is a large and engrossing subject. It is one of many into which we attempt in the present study to make a preliminary reconnaissance, in order to gain a fuller impression of the many facets of Baroque instrumental music than might be obtained from listening only to conventional modern performances of it.

Our plan of campaign, if I may remind you of it, is to build up a historical perspective to which we can relate the music. Continuing then with the ways and means, rather than the musical end-product, you are asked to make yourself familiar in the next section with the function and importance of the continuo: then, before reviewing the three main forms of Baroque instrumental composition, to consider the characteristics of the instruments of the period.

---

[1] You might be familiar with Elgar's own recording of his 'Enigma' variations, in which the strings make considerable use of portamento in their playing.

[2] *BH*, ii, 992.

The choir gallery of the Stadtkirche, Weimar, the frontispiece of J. G. Walther's Musicalisches Lexicon, Leipzig 1732 (British Museum)

3 THE CONTINUO

3.1 Background

By the sixteenth century compositions of great complexity were being written by Netherlanders and Italians, Englishmen and Spaniards: music in which the overall effect of joining voices together in many parts was being turned increasingly to expressive means. Such a polyphonic texture was constructed of individual voices of more or less equal importance. The feeling I get listening to a mass or motet by Palestrina, for example, or a madrigal by one of the many distinguished English and Italian composers of the late sixteenth century, is that the lines themselves are rather more important than the harmony created by fitting the voices together. Each line is carefully adapted to the text—often, even to the point of reflecting the natural intonation and emphasis of the spoken language. And each part is an attractive, clearly shaped melodic line of its own. The vertical combination is important, of course, but not more important than the individual lines, as it was to become in later music. However, towards the end of the century, particularly in the music of the Italian Gesualdo, and also in that of most of the English madrigalists, we find more and more that deliberate attempts are made to paint key words in the text a certain 'colour' by arranging that the individual lines may, at a point when the word is clearly heard, all combine to produce a telling harmony. They were discovering more about the potential of harmony as a means of creating interest in its own right. But in general the harmony has a half-accidental quality about it in Renaissance music.

Should you think I am putting it too strongly, you must, at all events, agree that harmonically there is a big difference between Renaissance and Baroque music. I'll explain why.

If you have come to this course having done the second level Arts course, *Renaissance and Reformation*, you will already be familiar with the characteristics of the Renaissance style in music. You will have read about, and listened to, Palestrina's *Missa Aeterna Christi munera*, Byrd's *Ave verum corpus*, vocal pieces by Monteverdi, Morley and Gibbons and keyboard music by Farnaby, Byrd, Gibbons and Sweelinck. It would be instructive to turn to units 17–19 of the course to remind yourself. Obviously, if you are not familiar with details of the style it would be particularly useful for you to buy or refer to these units at your study centre, to find out what I mean by talking about the accent in Renaissance music being on the 'horizontal' aspect of the music, the shape of each individual line, rather than on the 'vertical', the harmony produced at any point by piling up all the lines on top of one another.

The basic texture of Renaissance music was a polyphony of independent and more or less equal voices. I say 'more or less', because the uppermost parts tend to have more movement than the bass. In Baroque music there is a firm bass and a florid treble, shared by many parts, or, simply taken by one, all held together by unobtrusive harmony. And the harmony, far from having an accidental quality—of 'happening' because other more important things brought it about—now becomes highly systematized and in certain respects may be regarded as the most important element in the music. In fact the roles have been changed; now it is the melodies which have to 'happen' to go this way or that, and so we can say each part is a 'melodization' of the harmony. Since the harmony is heard complete anyway, played by the continuo, there is no harmonic loss—though there would of course be a loss of melodic interest—if some parts were missed out. Composers knew this, naturally, and the Italian G. B. Vitali, for example, indicated that a sonata for six melodic instruments and continuo in his *Varie Sonate, op. 11* ('various sonatas') could be reduced to 'il primo Violino solo e Violone' if desired.[1]

Now this emphasis in Baroque music on top and bottom was not new. It may be seen in the ballad of the Ars Nova, the early *frottola* of northern Italy, and the Burgundian *chanson* (both forerunners of the madrigal), as well as in the voice-plus-accompaniment of the *Elizabethan Ayre*.[2] And there are pieces by Orlando Gibbons (1583–1625) and Thomas Morley (1558–1603), for instance, which on account of the distribution of parts and the compass of the voices or instruments involved, resemble the accompanied duet and the trio sonata of the Baroque. But the essential differences between such Renaissance pieces and compositions in the new Baroque style are that, (i) in the Baroque, the top and bottom are cared for more obviously as the most important parts of the texture, and what happens in the range enclosed by them doesn't seem to concern the composer to the same extent, and (ii) in the Baroque, the bass is harmonically functional. Having written the top and the bottom, if he indicated in a special manner what the harmony was supposed to be, the composer could leave the inner parts to be supplied by musicians playing in the continuo—something the composer of Renaissance music could not do since the principle of the basso continuo had not been formulated then.

I do not need to remind you of the pitfalls in periodization, of applying a stylistic label and assuming that all music of the period was written in that style. Though we call the period from the beginning of the seventeenth century to the mid-eighteenth century 'Baroque', the beginnings and endings of the time when musicians generally adopted the Baroque style differed from centre to centre, country to country. There was quite an overlap at the end of the sixteenth and early seventeenth century when music was being composed in both styles. And well on into the seventeenth century composers of music which is ostensibly in the old style were being influenced in the actual process of composing by the new emphasis on top and bottom. It may be seen from the autograph of Henry Purcell's string fantasias in the British Museum, for example, that the top and bottom lines were done first, being in the same ink, while the middle parts in a different ink are not even always finished.

A useful indication of the rate of *general* acceptance of the basso continuo concept of composition is seen in the work of Claudio Monteverdi (1567–1643). In his eight books of madrigals we may see the transition from the Renaissance texture of independent and equal voices in polyphony to that of the Baroque emphasizing 'top and bottom'. The first four (1597–1603) are polyphonic; in the fifth and sixth books (1605, 1614), Monteverdi introduces the solo with continuo; the seventh and eighth books (1619, 1638) consist entirely of dramatic pieces with continuo.

The origins of the basso continuo are of less importance for the purposes of this study than the results of its adoption. We shall note only briefly, therefore, that towards the end of the sixteenth century some Italian musicians were dissatisfied with the polyphonic vocal style—mainly on account of the fact, they said, that nothing could be heard clearly because all the voices were constantly coming in across each other, repeating words, destroying the verbal sense and

---

[1] *SBE*, 59.

[2] For examples of lute ayres, listen to the record produced to accompany the units in the A201 course on Elizabethan poetry: A201 OU6.

generally making a confused (though exciting) noise. Their attempt to give the words a chance to be heard absolutely distinctly led to the monodic style (single voice with bass accompaniment), which was discovered to be an expressive and adaptable new medium. Experiments by members of the Florentine *Camerata*, a group of scholars and eminent artists of all kinds, who used to meet at the home of the wealthy *dilettante* Giovanni de' Bardi, realized the possibilities inherent in the new medium, and in their attempt to recreate the dramatic recitation of the ancient Greeks established the beginnings of *opera*, a development of tremendous importance which offered a whole new dimension in music. In this monodic style the singer was able to identify himself completely and convincingly with the character he was portraying; he could deliver his words in the most natural rhythm, to a deliberately simple melody. After centuries of contrapuntal music this was a powerful contrast in style, the emphasis being entirely on the one singer, who was given the advantage of harmonic and rhythmic support by such instruments as were available.

The continuo's origin in vocal music may be discerned in the following extract, from a 'Discourse on Ancient Music and Good Singing' (*c.* 1580), which, though attributed to Giovanni de' Bardi, may have been written by some other member of the *Camerata* (probably Vincenzo Galilei, father of the famous astronomer).

> the music of our time has two divisions—one which is called counterpoint and another which we shall call the art of good singing. The first of these is simply a combination of several melodies and of several modes sung at the same time.

Counterpoint, the author obviously felt to be unsuitable for vocal composition because, in his opinion, little was clearly heard. He continues with an amusing allusion:

> Messer Bass, soberly dressed in semibreves and minims, stalks through the ground-floor of his palace while Soprano, decked out in minims and [crotchets], walks hurriedly about the terrace at a rapid pace and Messers Tenor and Alto, with various ornaments and in habits different from the others, stray through the rooms of the intervening floors. For in truth it would seem a sin to the contrapuntists of today if all the parts were heard to beat at the same time with the same notes, with the same syllables of the verse, and with the same longs and shorts; the more they make the parts move, the more artful they think they are. This, in my opinion, is the concern of the stringed instruments, for, there being no voice in these, it is fitting that the player, in playing airs not suited to singing or dancing . . . should make the parts move and that he should contrive canons, double counterpoints, and other novelties to avoid wearying his hearers. And I judge this to be the species of music so much condemned by the philosophers, especially by Aristotle in the Eighth Book of his *Politics*, where he calls it artificial and wholly useless. . . .[1]

Giulio Caccini (c. 1550–1616) and Jacopo Peri (1561–1633), both Romans, became musicians at the Medici court in Florence. The earliest operas were composed by them: Peri's *Dafne* (now lost) in 1597 and *Euridice* (1600) by Peri with parts by Caccini, who then in the same year reset the whole text. Caccini uses the terms *basso continuato* and *basso seguente* in the preface to his *Euridice*.

[1] *SRMH*, 293–4.

In 1602 Lodovico Grossi da Viadana (1565–1627) of Mantua cathedral published a book of pieces with accompaniment for basso continuo: *Cento Concerti Ecclesiastici a 1, 2, 3, 4 e 5 voci con il Basso Continuo per Sonar nell'Organo* (a hundred church concertos for one to five voices with a basso continuo part for the organ). It was a work which had a lasting influence on the development of religious chamber music,[1] although its continuo part consists only of the bass notes, without any indication as to the harmony intended, which is a matter we must now consider.

3.2 Musical Shorthand: Figured Bass

In providing only the bass line to his *Cento Concerti Ecclesiastici* without any additional indication as to what the harmony should be, Viadana was not making an advance: organists, who seldom had the advantage of a score of the choral music they were performing, were used to fitting the harmony they felt to be most appropriate above the bass part of a composition. This was all right as long as they had reasonable time to get to know the music, and if it was not harmonically too unusual. But as an aid to ensuring the correct harmony (the right chord over the bass in *every* case) a musical shorthand evolved which, by means of signs and figures, indicated precisely what the harmony should be. In 1607 Agostini Agazzari, choirmaster at Siena cathedral, published a treatise in which he advocated the use of this new musical shorthand, and gave instructions in how to learn and apply it.

In order to show accurately how the 'flow of the harmony' is to be obtained— or, how the harmonic progression, as it is called, is formed—some indication is given to the player at every point where a new chord is introduced. To a great extent the system relies on the player knowing what notes comprise any chord which is intended. The system does not tell him at what octave he should play these notes, or whether he should sound the same note simultaneously at two or three pitches ('doubling' it). But more about that later. What it does is to assume that from his training as a musician he will know what notes belong to any chord.

The continuo player would know from the key signature and from the accidentals used which key the music he was playing was in. He also would feel from the tempo of the movement whether the harmony tended to change on every single beat or only on every strong beat. If no sign or figure was added above or below the bass note in his part, he would play a chord using the notes of the root position triad on that note, considered within the context of the scale in the key he was in. If one would expect the chord on a certain degree of the scale to be a minor chord, but wished a major chord to be played instead, this the player could easily provide if he saw the sharp sign added above or below the bass line. And similarly, any other alteration to the basic triad could be indicated. Chords other than the basic root position triads were indicated by adding numerals which gave the player the most important intervals comprised in those chords. The figure 6, for example, indicated that the chord contained a 6th. This the player knew to be a 'first inversion' chord: if the root position triad of C major (C–E–G) is turned upside down so that the C goes up to the top and E is now the bass note (E–G–C), it is called a first inversion.

[1] *Ibid.*, 419.

The figure 6 indicates the interval from the E up to the C which is a sixth. The full figuring should be $\frac{6}{3}$, to indicate the third from the E up to the G as well, but in practice the figure 6 was taken as sufficient. If the G of those three notes serves as the bass, then it is a 'second inversion', which, because these are the intervals counting up from the bass, is indicated by the figures $\frac{6}{4}$ added above or below the bass line.

2nd inversion

$\frac{6}{4}$

Again, recognizing that the figures indicate the most important intervals in each chord, the indication 4–3 tells the player that there is a suspension: the interval of a 4th, which was then regarded as a dissonance, was first to be played, then to be resolved on to the note a third above the bass.

4 3

I have only told you the beginning of the story as it were, and I know that if you have never done any harmony you will have found what I have just said difficult. If it is any consolation to you, many people find it a bit of a problem getting into this way of thinking about chords, and I should think it would have been even more difficult at the beginning of the Baroque era before harmony had been systematized (which became possible largely *as a result* of adopting the musical shorthand we are talking about). Certainly, something of the attitude towards harmony, and figured bass in particular—or 'thorough bass', as it was also called in England—may be seen in the title of this instruction book which was published in London in 1770. Robert Falkener's *Instructions for Playing the Harpsichord, wherein is fully explained the Mystery of Thorough Bass; with Divers other Material Things hitherto kept a Profound Secret by the Musical Society, To which is added, Exact Rules for Tuning the Harpsichord* (I like the 'last-but-not-least' which is offered!).

The system of notation is fairly simple: being able to 'realize' the harmony from the figured bass came with practice, and obviously some were better at it than others.

To use the shorthand figuring advocated by Agazzari meant putting the responsibility for spacing the harmony on the player. He had to decide how he was going to share out the notes of the chord under his fingers. Not all composers had such faith in the ordinary organist's ability to do this discreetly, and Emilio di Cavalieri (*c.* 1550–1602), another Roman who had been drawn to Florence, preferred to stipulate exactly in which part the suspension, for example, ought to take place. If he had written the 4–3 suspension I mentioned above, it should be taken exactly at those intervals of a fourth to a third above the bass note; the same harmonic effect, but with an octave plus a fourth and an octave plus a third between the bass and the suspension, would be figured 11–10, and with two octaves plus a fourth etc., between the bass and the suspended part, 18–17.

4 – 3   11 – 10   18 – 17

But this was far too cumbersome a method to gain support. Besides, one of the real advantages and attractions of figured bass is its flexibility. As long as the harmonic progression is clearly indicated (that is, the nature of each chord if the harmony were to be played simply as a succession of chords), the continuo might be played as most appropriate to the instruent or instruments available.

To be able to realize the figured bass with others required, obviously, that all the musicians had to be familiar with the same musical language. In the sixteenth century the variety of church modes that had been used for centuries were giving way to two modes in particular called the Ionian and Aeolian. These became known as *major* and *minor* modes, because in the Ionian the interval between the tonic and the third degree of the scale was a major third, and in the Aeolian a minor third. English musicians referred to them in the seventeenth and eighteenth centuries as the 'greater' and 'lesser' third. The experiments in accompanied monody and the introduction of the basso continuo, with its figured bass, coincided with a tendency towards an exclusive use of the major and minor modes, and of a new feeling for the expressive potential of harmony.

But harmony was not systematized in the Renaissance, although harmonic effects were certainly not engineered entirely accidentally. You may have observed in sixteenth-century music how the lowest part sometimes crosses over the next one above it for the sake of preserving the shape of a melodic figure in the line. In the music units of the *Renaissance and Reformation* course, a detailed study is made of 'The Silver Swan' by Orlando Gibbons. This offers a particularly good illustration of how the Second Bass and the part above it, the First Bass, cross. The First Bass momentarily becomes the lowest actual part for the sake of keeping a certain figure intact in each of these individual lines. The discussion of this beautiful part-song comes in pages 75–8 of the units (units 17–19) and the score of the whole piece is provided on pages 19 and 20 in the *Music Supplement* to these units. If you have access to these units, refer to the third bar of the piece and note the rising scale figure which passes from one part to another. It appears in the First Bass, then in the Alto, the Second Bass and then the First Bass again. The music is sung on the Renaissance Music record (Open University OUA 201) Side 1, Band 5. If you have difficulty in obtaining the second level material you can get this point *by looking* at the following quotation.

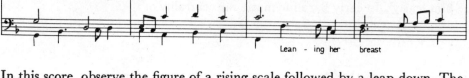

In this score, observe the figure of a rising scale followed by a leap down. The First Bass (with stems up—the Second Bass has stems down) drops an octave in b. 4 and lands on the same note as the bottom Bass. But by the time the First

Bass starts moving again, the Second Bass has already begun with the rising scale figure, leaving him behind as the real bass to the harmony.

This kind of crossing of lower parts happened also occasionally in keyboard music, but since the lower parts in the texture of a keyboard piece were not distinguished by individual timbres (as they were in a vocal ensemble) the result aurally was confusing, though it might look skilful on paper. So, during this late sixteenth-, early seventeenth-century period, there arose the concept of a bass that was no longer to be treated with the same freedom of movement as the parts above it, but which consisted of *all the actual lowest notes in the music*. This was the continuo. And extremely dull many of these parts were in the beginning.

3.3 Tonality and Harmonic Stability

The basso continuo brought a kind of order which Renaissance polyphony had lacked, although in its way this lack had been part of the beauty of the style. Music could still be contrapuntal—the ideals of the *Camerata* were not shared by everyone—but the contrapuntal lines had to fit in with the harmony which was at the same time being clearly stated by the continuo instruments.

In adopting the new shorthand of figures, composers were forced to become better aware of the harmonic implication of all the chords they used. It became second nature to them to jot down quickly over the bass note the figure or sign for the chord they intended, and in doing so they could not help but become more conscious of how the chords they chose 'worked' in relation to other chords.

This awareness was partly a result of the development of tonality, and at the same time it contributed to and strengthened the newly emerging tonal system. In this system every note and every chord has a particular relationship to all the others, and in any key (with its complementary major and minor modes), all the notes and chords tend to be used in ways which emphasize the centrality of the tonic around which they all turn, together with their own relationships to it.

Corelli's first set of sonatas was published in 1681, a useful date to remember since it indicates roughly the beginning of what is termed the 'late' or 'high' Baroque in music. Although the dates 1600–1750 broadly give the extent of the period in which composers were writing in a 'Baroque' style, a great deal can happen in a century and a half, and in the century and a half in question they did so quickly. On listening to, say, music by Caccini from the beginning of the period and that of J. S. Bach at the end, it becomes immediately obvious that they are strongly dissimilar in many respects. The most important feature shared by them is the continuo, and with it a certain kind of relationship between the continuo chord progression and the melodies above. Distinguishing them fundamentally is the function tonality plays in the music. To draw attention to the stylistic distinction between music in which the composer is still experimenting with tonality and music in which he has a complete grasp of it, Baroque music from Corelli onward is sometimes called 'late' Baroque, and the Baroque music before him 'early'. In early Baroque music the centrality of the tonic was mainly established through the use of the chords a fifth above it, the dominant, and a fifth below, the subdominant. Given the right context (and this is what composers were discovering), the dominant can be made to sound as if it strongly wants to move on to the tonic, and when this is repeated a number of times the tonic inevitably assumes more and more importance *as the tonal centre of the music*.

Exercise

Here is one way of proving it. Johann Pachelbel's *Canon*[1] for three violins and continuo is on Baroque Music II side 2 band 1. Throughout this piece, the same two-bar bass line is repeated without remission.

Above it, Pachelbel works a three-part canon. The parts begin at two-bar intervals, each repeating exactly what the part before it had played, at the same pitch. It is a strict form of composition, potentially a tedious one since the two-bar harmonic progression is to be repeated without alteration and the imitation in the violins continued without relief. Modulation, for the sake of variety, is thus not possible.

Listen to this piece, and decide what effect the unremitting repetition of the harmonic sequence has.

Play Baroque Music II side 2 band 1

My Comment

I find it has a hypnotic fascination which creates a satisfying feeling of inevitability. I know the progression after the second time; I know it begins with the tonic chord, and I look forward to hearing this chord. My expectation is raised each time I hear the 4th beat dominant chord.

And quickly I find myself looking forward to hearing *that* chord when the subdominant comes round.

These chords are the pillars of the tonal system, and by association and familiarity with their use in music generally I come to expect them to be used in certain ways—ways which tend to emphasize the tonality by 'pointing', as we have seen here, towards the tonic chord itself.

The overall effect, because Pachelbel is skilful in varying his melodic lines, is not tedious at all, and it is only with astonishment that I realize, when I have looked at the score, that the progression is repeated no less than twenty-eight times.

Increasing tonal awareness on the part of the composer, assisted by his acceptance of a shorthand language for indicating the chord required for the harmony, led to the establishment of a system of *functional harmony* in which not only the dominant and subdominant but all other accepted chords were able directly or indirectly to 'point' towards the tonic and emphasize it as the tonal centre of the music. Similarly, composers discovered how to use modulations to the dominant *key* and other keys to emphasize the tonic key as the tonal centre in the course of longer movements.

By the end of the eighteenth century, as a result of many treatises on the subject, and conventions in the music they wrote, composers had become conscious of the function of the harmonic elements they were handling. Thus the tonal system

---

[1] See *NDM* for an explanation of canon if you are not sure what it means.

was so well understood that there was no longer any real *need* to have the harmonic tread sounding in order to keep the other parts to the straight and narrow, as it were. Even so, although the basso continuo was redundant, the habit died hard and, as we shall see, it continued in the person of the keyboard accompanist well on into the nineteenth century.

The practice of learning how to handle chords by harmonizing figured basses on paper has never really died out. Although this method has been much frowned upon—possibly because the Victorians swore by it—textbooks like Ebenezer Prout's *Harmony, Its Theory and Practice* (1889) may still be found very useful, in fact.

The continuo was the distinguishing feature of music in the Baroque style: it appeared in all kinds of composition—we will be looking at the very rare exceptions, like duets and unaccompanied sonatas, later. But it is important to realize that practically all Baroque music needs a continuo section: instruments in the ensemble to play both the bass notes and the harmonies indicated. So, whether it is dance music, a trio sonata, a concerto, opera or oratorio, the continuo should always be heard stating the harmonic tread of the piece. The word 'continuo' ought to remind you, anyway, of the character of the part conventionally written: it 'continues' from beginning to end, often non-stop. It also used to be known as *thorough bass* and *through bass* in England, the harmonic foundation of the music which goes on throughout. Other terms for it are: *General-Bass* (German), *Basse chiffrée* (i.e. figured) and *Basse continue* (French) in addition to the Italian terms mentioned already.

Sextet by Louis Michel van Loo, 1768 (Hermitage Museum)

3.4 Continuo Instruments

Baroque music was thoroughly practical. Its firm feet-on-the-ground practicality distinguishes music of the age of the basso continuo from what followed. Like the nineteenth century, for example, the period saw a great deal of theorizing about all aspects of musical composition and performance, even the nature of music itself. But there was a difference: the Romantic composer's music was precisely orchestrated and, if he had the self-confidence of a Wagner, he would not willingly allow a note to be altered or any detail to deviate in performance from what he had committed to his final score. The eighteenth-century Kapellmeister, on the other hand, developed resourcefulness as a matter of necessity, and had a refreshingly open attitude towards the selection and number of instruments which participated as available in the ensemble music he directed.

Nowhere is this more obvious than with respect to the essential function of contributing to the continuo itself.

But, as long as instrumental music was dependent upon a basso continuo for its harmonic stability, the individual qualities of the instruments concerned in playing the continuo were unlikely to be shown to the best possible advantage. Agazzari listed in his *Del sonare sopra il basso* ('Of playing upon a bass with all instruments and of their use in the consort'), 1607, the instruments in general use in the early seventeenth century, which might be divided into two classes,

> namely, into instruments like a foundation and instruments like ornaments. Like a foundation are those which guide and support the whole body of the voices and instruments of the consort; such are the organ, harpsichord, etc., and similarly, when there are few voices or solo voices, the lute, theorbo, harp, etc. Like ornaments are those which, in a playful and contrapuntal fashion, make the harmony more agreeable and sonorous, namely, the lute, theorbo, harp, *lirone*, cithern, spinet, *chitarrino*, violin, pandora, and the like.[1]

The continuo began as a very mixed collection of instruments in the formative years of the Baroque style, and, since plucked instruments, particularly the theorbo and the lute, were at the height of fashion then, they were naturally used. By the end of the seventeenth century the use of a keyboard instrument had come to be regarded as indispensable in the continuo, though other instruments might be added to it as resources permitted.

There was, in addition, a fundamental problem in that all the instruments were not tuned to the same system and consequently, even if the players each played their own instrument perfectly correctly as far as they themselves were concerned, when they all sounded together the tuning was imperfect. The older instruments, of the lute and viol families, were tuned in equal temperament, while the keyboard instruments, the harp and the new family of unfretted string instruments, the violins, used mean-tone temperament. The intonation of wind instruments was sufficiently poor and variable as to allow these to belong to either camp. You must turn to your set book *A New Dictionary of Music*, the *Oxford Companion to Music* or any longer reference work for an explanation of these terms, but what it meant in effect was that 'never the twain shall meet'—or at least, it was not advisable, even with professional players. A glance at the lute on plate 15 of *MI* will help you realize how problems of intonation

---

[1] *SRMH*, 424. Refer to *MI* for details of these instruments. Agazzari's *chitarrino* was presumably a smaller-scaled chitarrone.

were likely to be acute, and to see what Handel's friend and rival Johann Mattheson meant by writing in 1713,

> should you meet a lute-player eighty years old, you may rest assured he has been *tuning* sixty years of this; and the worst is, that amongst a hundred players, particularly amongst amateurs, you will find scarcely two who can tune correctly.[1]

By the late seventeenth century it had become conventional for the bass line to be melodic in its own way, and experience showed that an ideal combination for playing the continuo consisted of either the organ or the harpsichord, together with a single-line instrument to reinforce the bass by etching out the contour of the bass line itself. The bassoon was frequently employed in larger groups, and also when the melody instruments were wind instruments (in a trio sonata for flute, oboe and continuo for instance); but the instruments most often referred to specifically are the viola da gamba and cello. The treble and tenor viols had fallen out of common use by the end of the seventeenth century and, as you will see in the second television programme of the course, the string section of the orchestra at this time was noticeably comprised of new and old elements: the new, violins and violas, at the top and the old, the viola da gamba and violone, still very much in evidence at the bottom. The cello and double bass were also being used, and were to become increasingly common in orchestral music in the eighteenth century.

The question of which instruments might best play the continuo would not have troubled the court orchestra or the Gentlemen's Music Club in the eighteenth century. It would have been taken by the most competent of suitable instrumentalists available, notwithstanding the name of the part. A music club always had a harpsichord, except when it met in a room with a small organ in it. At court, the Kapellmeister might have more than one harpsichord, and an organ in the concert room as well. When such a selection of keyboard instruments was at hand it became possible to perform concerti grossi in a way that emphasized the tonal contrast between the small solo group and the orchestral reinforcement.

That composers had this kind of treatment in mind is shown by the fact that separate continuo parts are sometimes written for the two distinct sections of the orchestra; one keyboard instrument to accompany the solo group, and another to play with the ripieno. Handel, for example, writes for two in his op. 6 concertos, and a useful distinction may also be seen in the concertos of William Corbett (died in 1748), who allocates parts—both of which are figured—to 'Organo o Violoncello', and 'Cembalo o Basso Ripieno'. If the concertino is supported by the mellow tone of a chamber organ and the ripieno given the advantage of the incisiveness and weight of a large harpsichord, the effect is particularly attractive, though in practice of course the one instrument could serve adequately on its own. Concerto performances with two keyboard instruments in separate continuo sections, however, were probably a luxury enjoyed only at the larger courts. The smaller music club would have the part headed 'Organo' played on its modest harpsichord, interpreting 'Organo' in the same way as the author of *The Delightful Pocket Companion for the German Flute*, a collection of tunes with a dictionary of musical terms appended published in about 1745 (John Simpson, London), to mean

> properly an Organ, but when it is written over any Piece of Musick, then it signifies the Thorough Bass.

---

[1] In the translation by F. Praeger of Emil Naumann *History of Music* (London, Cassell, n.d. 1886), iii, 624.

From what you have read and heard of the organ and harpsichord in the foregoing units of this course and earlier Open University Arts Courses, you should appreciate that the keyboard player would almost certainly wish to realize his continuo part quite differently according to whether he were at a large organ, a little chamber organ, or a harpsichord. What he did would be influenced by the liveliness of the acoustics of the room or building in which the music was being performed. The style of his realization could have a noticeable effect on the performance, and similarly, the same piece of music played by various assortments of continuo instruments can sound remarkably different. This you can hear in the second television programme of the course, when a Corelli trio sonata movement is played with a viola da gamba and chittarone on the continuo, then repeated with a harpsichord and cello.

The much-travelled German composer, Georg Muffat (*c.* 1645–1704), who had learned the French style at first hand in Paris, and the Italian from none other than Corelli himself in Rome, makes some observations relevant to our discussion of the basso continuo in the Foreword to his collection of concertos published in Passau in 1701.

For performances with only a few musicians he recommends that the bass should be played by a small-sized bass rather than a large double bass, 'and to this may be added, for the greater ornamentation of the harmony, a harpsichord or theorbo, played from the same part'. When more musicians are available, Muffat says, they should be added to the ripieno, and

> In this case, to make the harmony of the bass the more majestic, a large double bass will prove most serviceable.

And when there is no shortage of players at all, they might be put to reinforce the ripieno even further, 'ornamenting (the bass) with the accompaniment of harpsichords, theorbos, harps, and similar instruments'.[1]

3.5 Baroque View of the Bass

The idiomatic distinctions between the harpsichord, organ, lute, harp, guitar, 'cello, viola da gamba, violone, double bass, bassoon and trombone could not be accommodated in a part which was in most cases seen only as providing a clear harmonic foundation to the ensemble and *not* a particular tone colour.

Many composers cultivated the art of writing interesting bass lines. A glance at the variety of bass lines in units 10–11 will show this—and you can listen to these pieces on the record. But the bass was not expected to be melodic in the same kind of way as the top parts: its function was considered more important all the same, for in Baroque music the harmonic progression, before all else, had to be faultless.

The harmonic progression has to be faultless in other styles of music, of course, but it is particularly important in this style because the progression counts for more than the 'embroidery' of it in the upper parts. Freely moving treble parts were of secondary importance, so much so that players felt little compunction about altering them, embellishing the given line with added runs and ornaments. As you have read, although the composer wrote a part precisely, he knew he would not hear it played exactly as he had intended it and written it down. But, he could expect a good musician to play *an approximation* of his,

[1] *SRMH*, 450–1.

deriving the main notes of the melody from the chords of the harmonic progression which was plainly stated by the instruments of the continuo.

This seems all wrong to us since we are used to fixing our attention to the melody, and thinking little of the bass line except when a bad progression annoys us. The general attitude in the Baroque, nevertheless, was that a composition stood or fell as much by its bass line as by the appeal of its melodies.

Here is a definition from Grassineau's *Musical Dictionary*, published in 1740:

> *Bass*: that part of a concert which is most heard, which consists of the gravest and deepest sounds, and which is played on the largest pipes or strings of a common instrument, as of an Organ, Lute. . . . Musicians hold the *Bass* to be the principal part of the concert, and the foundation of the composition; though some will have the *Treble* the chief part, which others only make an ornament.

This definition was still being held at the end of the Baroque period in England thirty years later, as we see in John Hoyle's *Dictionarium Musica* [*sic*], of 1770. In addition to what Grassineau said, worded slightly differently, Hoyle states:

> [The Bass is] the foundation of Harmony; for which reason it is a maxim among Musicians, that where the Bass is good the harmony is seldom bad.

Yet, although the bass was functionally the most important part, it was, as we have seen, left to chance precisely which instruments, and how many, should take care of it. Of course, each of these players had to adapt the bass part, and to suit the harmony which he derived from the musical shorthand in figures to the compass of his own instrument. So in addition to the instruments playing the melodic lines at the top of the instrumental texture and those actually sounding the written bass line, there would be others improvising parts which fitted in with the harmony—which, since they were improvised, meant that the music sounded slightly, if not markedly, different every time it was performed.

According to the seventeenth-century English musician Roger North, the sound of the continuo should 'fill and strike the audience as with a whip; as if there were devinity in the sound, able to excite their spirits into profesy. This no soft noise, tho' in its place [it] is good, can doe.'

The same writer commented on the volume which Nicola Matteis could get out of a guitar, playing with 'force upon it to stand in consort against an harpsichord'.[1] Both statements imply that musicians then had a rather different view of balance from ours, that modern performances of Baroque music should have heavier, louder, more prominent continuo sections than we usually hear at present.

The bass was not expected to be melodic in the sense that an upper part is tuneful. It had to be shaped differently on account of its harmonic requirements, but also it had less rhythmic flexibility. At least one element of the music had to maintain a regular and uncomplicated metre, and this fell to the continuo. In consequence, one of the distinctive characteristics of much Baroque music is the striding bass line, which continues from beginning to end with little or no rhythmic change. Roger North called it a *basso andante* ('walking bass'), and explained his liking for movements with this kind of bass,

---

[1] *NOM*, 274 and 357.

it expresseth steddyness of mind, not affected or altered by the *cantabile* of the upper parts. And it humours a voice most exquisitely; for that is always melodious, and moves with a self-regard, as if unconcerned with what waits upon it. And the stepps of the base make out the time, which is not in the voice distinguishable, and that is a constant vertue of it; for it keeps the time of the whole consort and all fall into just measures with it; as one may fancy a rider singing finely while his horse trotts the time.

Exercise

Listen to the following movements, without referring to the scores, and decide which of them does *not* have a continuo line of the kind North called a 'walking bass'.

Corelli *Concerto grosso op. 6 no. 8*, Allegro 2nd movement
Leclair *Sonata op. 5 no. 6* 'Le Tombeau', Grave
J. S. Bach *Suite in B Minor*, Polonaise
Ariosti *Lesson in A* for viola d'amore, Adagio

Answer

The Leclair.

My Comment

Although the Corelli is fast, its bass continues with regular movement throughout, in contrast to the melodic dialogue above. The bass of the Bach Polonaise is almost entirely regular again, but when we come to the middle section we lose this, of course, because the tune is in the bass. The Ariosti also provides a good illustration for North's rider singing finely while his horse trots the time.

3.6 Practical Matters

Pictures of instrumental groups tell us that, compared with the usual modern arrangement of the orchestra, with the cellos on one side and the double basses tucked away at the back, in the seventeenth and eighteenth centuries the instruments of the basso continuo were conventionally placed in a more advantageous position: up in the front with the other instruments around them.

Obviously players had to fit in where best there was room, but the ensemble benefited if all the players were able to sit fairly close to the instruments which were playing the basic line of the composition. This was not primarily for the sake of co-ordination, although undoubtedly it is easier to play exactly together if all can hear the harpsichord lead clearly, but so that no one should be in doubt as to the harmonic progression of which each part was a melodization.

Instructions to precisely this effect—though this time they are singers, not instrumentalists—are given in the *Rudiments of Music* by the Scottish music publisher, Robert Bremner. In a thoroughly practical section headed *A plan for teaching a Croud*, he advises choirmasters on arranging the congregation:

> Having assigned all of them their Parts, place the Trebles on your right hand, the Counters [i.e. counter-tenors or altos] on your left, the Basses fronting you, and the Tenors behind them. By the Bass being thus in the Centre, the other Parts, which all arise from it, are equally supported.[1]

[1] Robert Bremner, *Rudiments of Music* (2nd ed., 1762), 57.

If this is borne in mind, it becomes doubly obvious that a keyboard instrument should be included in the orchestra for any performance of an eighteenth-century orchestral piece in Baroque style today.

The use of a keyboard instrument was not restricted to Baroque works; it belongs to the *galant* style as well. The continuo player at the keyboard, who was such an indispensable member of the Gentlemen's Subscription concert, had (by tradition) in many groups assumed the directorship of the ensemble—the responsibility professionally vested at court in the Kapellmeister.

It was natural, even after amateur music clubs of this kind had declined with the demise of the Baroque style, that the continuo harpsichordist should keep his place in the professional orchestra to give leads and fill in missing parts if he could. A continuo part is seldom provided for use in *galant* symphonies (look out for this in units 12–17: how many of the symphonies discussed have a figured bass?). The keyboard player, who towards the late eighteenth century was transferring from the harpsichord to the piano, had therefore to improvise from the cello and bass part, or, if necessary, a copy of the first violin part. Orchestral scores were almost unknown at this time, and they certainly were not generally available. Nevertheless, some concertos do have a figured bass, even though they are *galant* works. This supports the literary evidence, which shows that long after the end of the Baroque era the keyboard instrument was considered absolutely essential for the orchestra's stability—even though no part was written specifically for it. This was not only for the sake of ensuring harmonic completeness—which, since the keyboard player did not have a score, could not be ensured anyway—but in order to mark the rhythmic accentuation of the music and to give a general lead. This, the continuo's second function, became increasingly important as the music played became progressively more technically demanding for the performers.

In view of all of this, it is no accident that the definitive statement on the use of the keyboard instrument in orchestral music should date from the very time when the Baroque style was being superseded by the more dramatic and technically more difficult *galant* music. In the second part of his *Essay on the True Art of Playing Keyboard Instruments* (Berlin, 1762), Carl Philipp Emanuel Bach asserts [italics added]:

> no piece can be well performed without some form of keyboard accompaniment. Even in heavily scored works, such as operas performed out of doors, where no one would think that the harpsichord could be heard, *its absence can certainly be felt.* And from a position above the performers all of its tones are clearly perceptible. I base these observations on experience which may be duplicated by anyone.[1]

The idea of a keyboard accompaniment to a symphony strikes us as odd: we are not used to it (unless we have experienced it in incomplete school orchestras). Yet, it is a characteristic of music of the period more than adequately substantiated historically. Haydn, inconceivable though it may seem, was engaged by Salomon to 'preside at the piano' when his new symphonies were played in London in 1791–2 and 1794–5, and at the rival establishment, the Professional Concerts, Pleyel did the same.[2] (We do not know how much or what Haydn did, but he was there at the keyboard in the capacity of director of the orchestra.) Coming down to a less exalted level, the composer John Ross was organist and harpsichord player from 1783 to 1801 at the Musical Society of

---

[1] C. P. E. Bach, *Essay on the True Art of Playing Keyboard Instruments.* Part 2, para. 7 of the Introduction (modern edition trans. and ed. by W. J. Mitchell, Cassell, London, 1951), 173.

[2] Adam Carse, *The Orchestra in the XVIIIth Century*, 91–2.

A Music Party at Melton Constable in 1734, by D. Heins (Collection Lady Hastings, Melton Constable; Photo for Norwich Castle Museum by Hallam Ashley)

Aberdeen, and Charles Burney, the music historian, was appointed in about 1790 harpsichordist and director of the 'New Concerts' which had been established at the King's Arms, Cornhill, one of the many musical taverns in London which I mentioned earlier.

In music of the *galant* style particular attention was paid to instrumental colour, and all the parts were precisely scored. As a result, the various instruments which had been numbered with greater or lesser anonymity in the continuo were freed, to be developed in the roles for which they were best suited. So bassoons, on occasion, became tenor instruments, with a share of solos. The cello's upper register was shown to good effect, and the double bass was regarded as indispensable in the newly enlarged orchestra. It was a welcome emancipation of the orchestra's bass instruments. At the same time, because music was now written for specific instruments, it meant an end to the *ad hoc* participation by the plucked instruments, lute, guitar and harp, which in the early eighteenth century still contributed, if only infrequently, in continuo playing.

This awakening to the niceties of instrumental colour, and the exploration of possible combinations will be dealt with in tracing the development of the symphony, in units 12 to 17. The new taste for colourful orchestration had a positive effect on the major form of Baroque large-scale music, the concerto. When in the nineteenth century the concerto emerged from a slight decline in popularity in favour of the symphony in a new 'Soloist against the Orchestra' form, it was ideally suited to the temperament of the age, its multifarious orchestral colours painting the mood and providing a shifting back-cloth before which the soloist appeared to the best advantage. But such developments came to maturity in the period to which we have deliberately chosen to pay least attention in this particular course. Nevertheless, it was necessary, to get a view of the continuo and of what evolved out of it, to take our account into the nineteenth century.

3.7 The Keyboard Player as Soloist

Some composers obviously regarded the continuo more imaginatively than others, and it is as a direct result of this that certain new kinds of composition came into being. Right at the beginning of the sonata's history, Biagio Marini wrote for obligatory harpsichord (1626), and in some sonatas more than others in the seventeenth century the continuo contributed melodically, as well as serving its normal harmonic function. In the early eighteenth century, J. S. Bach's continuo writing is so attractive in itself that it is no surprise to find the usual Baroque solo with continuo support developing into a balanced partnership. In the sonatas for violin and harpsichord, for example, the harpsichord part is fully written out (not simply a figured bass) and contributes just as much as the stringed instrument. In the fifth of the *Brandenburg Concertos*, also, the normally concealed authority of the harpsichordist is revealed openly; from what sounds like a conventional concerto texture there quickly emerges a concertino harpsichord part, which in fact takes over as the main soloist in the piece. From such precedents as these sprang the Classical duo and the piano concerto. It is not important whether these examples taken from Bach's music were the earliest of their kind or not. The idea was in the air in the early eighteenth century, and it was inevitable that the keyboard instrument should assume greater importance as a soloist, both in chamber and larger-scale music.

The organ concerto was a common form of composition in England, particularly from the 1730s and '40s on, but Bach's *Fifth Brandenburg Concerto* (1721) was not published until the early nineteenth century, and so would not have been known to such writers as Felton, Avison, Burgess and Mudge, or even Handel, who gave these Englishmen the lead with brilliant performances of his own organ concertos. Nor would the concertos of these gentlemen, most of them written in the Baroque style at a time when continental composers were taking to the brighter *galant* style, possibly have been known to the composers whose piano concertos preceded Mozart's.

Promotion in the status of the keyboard instrument was bound to come, and of course it did. With increasing attention being paid to the piano, as the century drew to a close, the harpsichord and organ dropped out of concert use in favour of this latest, most versatile and fashionable keyboard instrument.

3.8 Realizing the Figured Bass

During the age of the continuo the ability to play from figured bass was essential for every keyboard player, as well as being very desirable in other instrumentalists. As you would expect, there was quite a market in textbooks on figured bass, ranging from the 'translation' of figures into simple chords (much the same kind of thing as the modern guitar tutor book giving the various chords in a diagrammatic form which shows the finger positions), to erudite treatises on the niceties of interpreting the figures to produce the most artistic accompaniment possible, such as the book by Carl Philipp Emanuel Bach already mentioned.

Here is an excerpt from the former kind of 'chord translation' book, James Hook's *Guida di Musica op. 75* (1794).

More recently we have seen a revival of the almost lost art of harpsichord playing. It is clear from eighteenth-century writings on the matter that opinions differed as to how, in general, the harpsichordist ought to contribute to the music once he is in the ensemble. The artistry with which he took the role of player-composer had an important bearing on the way the other musicians were likely to interpret their parts. He should not, like the least interesting of children, only be seen and not heard. On the other hand, he had to remember that although he was indispensable, he was to provide what in effect was an *accompaniment* to the melodic parts. Comments by historians of the period (Burney felt particularly qualified to pass astringent criticisms on this) show plainly that excessive prominence on the part of the harpsichordist was not desirable—especially if he allowed a facile technique to get the better of his discretion.

You will have an opportunity of hearing and seeing the normal combinations of instruments in the continuo section, in the music we play in the Baroque music television programmes (except for programme 4). Hearing them, you will probably be interested to know what kind of parts the continuo instrumentalists are playing: how much is written down, and how much has either been improvised or worked out from the instructions left by the composer. By way of answering your inquiry beforehand, but recognizing that this is not the place to embark on the theory of musical shorthand, here is a glimpse at the continuo part of one of the trio sonatas from which a movement is included on record.

It is the first Allegro of the very fine trio sonata which is part of J. S. Bach's *Musical Offering*. I will not say anything about it now, but want you to look at the score, which is in unit 10, and follow it as you listen.

The movement is on Baroque Music II, side 1 band 4. Note, that when you have followed the music through to the end of the score, you go back to the sign at bar 12 and continue from there to *Fine* ('The End').

Listen particularly to what the harpsichord is doing.

Play Baroque Music II side 1 band 4

What you have been following is of course a score of all the parts. In the performance of such a trio sonata in the eighteenth century the harpsichord player would not have had the luxury of a score of this kind, only a figured bass part.

Besides being an extremely adaptable means of providing the harmonic tread, the figured bass was incomparably economic in conveying most of the essential information in very little space. It did not give the melodic leads, but since the manner in which instruments or voices entered was done in a fairly conventional way, with which everyone was familiar, that did not matter.

It would not be possible for the harpsichordist to correct the flautist's part by looking at the figured bass, if in rehearsal the players felt that something was wrong in the way the articulation, or the grouping of a certain figure, was printed. But if a printing error occurred in the number of bars' rest, or in the notes given, this would usually be spotted fairly easily because whatever the flautist played would contradict the information provided by the figures and signs on the harmony to be expected. The flute and violin parts are a melodization of the harmony which is being played in a more basic, less contrapuntal form, on the harpsichord. Any clashes with the 'official' harmony on the harpsichord will obviously stick out. Instead of reading from a score, the harpsichordist has all he needs in this very short part: the figured bass for the whole of a sonata or a concerto is often printed on one side of only one page in eighteenth-century editions. You would be reminded on seeing such a short but 'informative' part, that the figured bass was a musical shorthand which could be written out very quickly.

Figured bass is a mystery only to the uninitiated. It is a shorthand which is not difficult to learn once one has a good working knowledge of how chords are formed. It is based, as you have already heard, on indicating the interval from the bass note to the next notes above in the chord, or, if it is a particular kind of dissonant chord, indicating the intervals which distinguish it. But, if the harmony intended is simply a root-position chord (on that degree of the scale) in the main key of the movement, then usually no figure at all is given.

Look at the score of that movement again. All Bach wrote for the continuo was the bass line with figures and signs appended to it.

Any harpsichordist might play his 'realization' of this and, if he is competent, the harmony should be exactly the same as we have on the recording. But there is much more to it than simply getting the harmony correct: the fullness of the harmony, the placing of the chords, the amount of movement and the kind of texture aimed at, are aspects of keyboard continuo playing on which we are glad to have the guidance of an eighteenth-century musician. In this case, we have. One of Bach's pupils, Johann Philipp Kirnberger (1721–83), left this realization of the figured bass. We will consider what happens here briefly, not in order to learn how it is done, but to gain an impression of what is involved.

Let's look at the first two bars of the movement

Observe, in 'slow motion', what the continuo player takes in at a glance and reacts to instinctively.

Bach's first bass note is C. The movement has a key signature of three flats: we know the harmony required is therefore the tonic chord of C minor

Kirnberger spaces out the notes which are available to him from the C minor triad thus,

The next bass note

requires the note at an interval of a 6th above it

and, to complete the chord, the note D. Although it is not given a numeral we know it is implied—as explained in 3.2. The chord is the first inversion of G

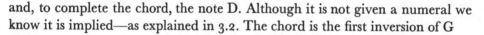

root   first
position inversion

Kirnberger spaces it out thus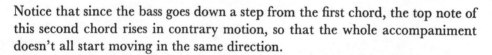

Notice that since the bass goes down a step from the first chord, the top note of this second chord rises in contrary motion, so that the whole accompaniment doesn't all start moving in the same direction.

The next bass note has no figure: we know it has to be the root-position chord of G major or minor. We are in the key of C minor, and the chord on the dominant of this key, G, is *major*, as all dominants are, so this one is G major. Look for the accidental required to confirm that the B flat of the key signature has to be raised to a B natural. We have just had it in the previous bass note and the accidental applies for the rest of the bar, though to prevent any mistakes by the player, Kirnberger writes in a B♮ in the right hand part since we have not had a B♮ at this pitch yet.

The next bass note indicates the chord of C minor, the tonic chord again,

while the numeral 6 modified by a natural (♮) indicates that instead of the interval of a sixth which the key signature would impose the B flat became B natural.

The third note of the triad, which as in the second chord of the movement is not indicated by a figure, is F. Kirnberger also has the G from the previous chord sounding at this point, thus making a dissonance which is not indicated in the notation.

The remaining two quavers

indicate C minor harmony, changing position from the first inversion to root position. Kirnberger simply holds the harmony in the right hand—so avoiding movement in both hands on every quaver, which can produce a monotonous and irritating 'chop-chop-chop' effect, with the

harpsichord's incisive attack separating each subdivision of the beat.

Exercise

In order to see the movement now from the continuo player's viewpoint, listen to it again, following this time Kirnberger's realization of the figured bass.

1 What sort of texture is established, how many parts? 2 What kind of melodies are there? 3 Does the continuo part cover a wide range or is it confined to a particular compass? 4 Are the right and the left hand treated more or less the same? 5 Do you feel this part supports the flute and violin adequately or, possibly, does it compete too strongly with them for your attention?

Play Baroque Music II side 1 band 4

Realization by J. P. Kirnberger of the figured bass of the second-movement
Allegro in J. S. Bach's trio sonata from *The Musical Offering*

Adagio Allegro

Dal Segno

My Comments

1 Although the number of actual notes heard at any time is usually four it is not a four-part texture. Rather, it is the bass, and a handful of notes for right hand. The bass line is allowed to move freely and clearly, without being smothered or crowded out by other parts too close to it.

2 There is no attempt at shaping a top-line melody; the right hand is treated as if of secondary importance to the left, concerning itself with held chords or suspensions, or giving rhythmic point to the movement.

3 The right hand keeps very much to the same compass all the way through— with the highest note of the handful rising and falling within a limited range of only a fourth or a fifth most of the time.

4 There is more movement, most of the time, in the bass than in the right hand.

5 When I listen to the movement I am struck by the great freedom of the two melodic parts, which move over a wide range supported all the while by this

70

rather static texture in the harpsichord part. Yes—I do feel it supports them adequately without competing too strongly against them.

Having observed here in 'slow motion' what the keyboard player might do in 'realizing' the bass—by taking a look at a few bars of Kirnberger's realization of Bach's figured bass in this movement—and having listened in particular to the harpsichord, you could profitably do the same with some of the other movements recorded.

Exercise

Bearing in mind the points you looked for in Kirnberger's realization of a figured bass, comment on the harpsichord parts of the following movements. The scores are all in unit 10, and the recordings as listed are all on Baroque Music II.

1 Telemann *Quartet sonata in D major* (Prelude) side 1 band 8
2 Rameau *Pièces de clavecin* ('La Livri') side 1 band 6
3 Ariosti *Lesson in A major for viola d'amore* side 2 band 7
4 Leclair *Sonata op. 5 no. 6* ('Le Tombeau') side 2 band 5

My Comments

1 The Telemann quartet Prelude is headed *Vivement* (lively), and the bass line is an active one. Like the Kirnberger this realization of the figured bass consists of a single line bass with an appropriate handful of notes in the right hand. The right-hand part is not quite as limited in range as in Kirnberger's realization and unlike the latter, contributes a snatch of melodic interest in the course of its unmelodic sequence of chords (bars 50–1).

2 This is not a realization of a figured bass, but a fully written-out harpsichord part. The differences between this and the Kirnberger realization, for instance, which should have struck you are: (i) the harpsichord in the Rameau is obviously a melodic participant not merely the provider of harmonic support. (ii) Hence the harpsichord part is flexibly written with many changes of texture, it covers a wide range, and it is rhythmically varied. (iii) A small amount of ornamentation is incorporated in the harpsichord part.

3 The bass of the Ariosti is not figured; it was left to the harpsichordist to fill in the harmony as he felt appropriate to the context. This realization, which is light and delicate, allows the viola d'amore soloist to play very gently and quietly. This instrument can be made to sound loud and strident, and had this been the player's approach to the piece the continuo realization would have needed to have been heftier, and much fuller. As it is, an appropriate balance is obtained. The right-hand part makes some melodic contributions (bars 6–8, 10).

4 The harpsichord deliberately plays a supporting role in this Leclair sonata; it does not compete with the violin in melodic interest, nor attempt to play above it in pitch. The violin plays almost entirely in double stopping (playing on two strings at once), so the harmonic effect is unusually rich even before the harpsichord realization of the figured bass is added. As the movement is slow, it is appropriate that the realization contributes to the effect of richness by means of some contrapuntal movement in the right-hand part (bars 6–10 for instance).

I hope that in considering the harpsichord parts of these movements you may have become better aware of what is involved, both in technique and taste, in the realization of continuo parts. Now, armed with a slice of period background and having made an acquaintance with the fundamental characteristic of Baroque music—the continuo—it is time we looked at the instruments which were used in music-making at this time.

Sainte Cecile, by Dominiquin. The instrument is a modified gamba (Louvre; Photo Bulloz)

4 INSTRUMENTS

To work through this section you will need *Musical Instruments through the Ages* edited by Anthony Baines (Penguin Books 1961), which is referred to as *MI*.

4.1 The Violin

By the late seventeenth century the violin was already a musical instrument of over a hundred years' standing, and fine violins of exceptional tonal quality were being made. The period in which we are interested at present, covering the late seventeenth and first half of the eighteenth centuries, saw the craft of violin-making reach a degree of excellence, particularly in Italy, unequalled anywhere before or since. This peak in the achievement of violin-makers coincided with the emergence of strong schools of violin-playing, as we have noted in the foregoing sections. Corelli and his contemporaries, as performers and teachers, by reputation and by the spread of their music, greatly stimulated interest in the violin and its music. Equally, the fact that exceptionally responsive and good-looking instruments were being made just then, and were available to people who could pay for them, contributed to establishing national and local schools of violin playing.

A good instrument does something for a good performer. There even comes a point—you have possibly experienced this yourself—when to progress to greater technical and musical maturity as a performer the acquisition of a better-quality instrument becomes essential. That Corelli and his contemporaries had in their hands the finest violins the world has ever known certainly influenced the direction in which music developed during the Baroque period. The emphasis was definitely on the violin, and most of the best purely instrumental music was written for it. Violin virtuosos captivated their audiences by technical feats of daring and brilliance, and by the sound they produced. To accommodate these qualities, there emerged the various forms of sonata and concerto.

Since the eighteenth century, composers have continued to write sonatas and concertos, and the technical competence of string players in general has unquestionably become greater than it was then. It is futile to argue whether the big names of today are better violinists than, say, Heifetz in the present century, Joachim, a contemporary of Brahms in the late nineteenth century, Paganini and Spohr earlier on, or Viotti, Tartini, Locatelli and back to Corelli. You would have to define very precisely what you were comparing and on what basis you were judging them. But going on *technical* requirements alone, the virtuosity of solo performers is now higher than it ever has been, with students and aspiring concert performers playing works such as the violin concertos by Elgar and Tchaikovsky, Sibelius, Berg and Bartok, and coping even with the monumental technical obstacles encountered in the Schoenberg violin concerto (despairingly said to have been written for a six-fingered violinist—and certainly much more demanding than the music we will be looking at in this course).

There has been a continuing advance in the ability of violinists to play more notes per second, over a greater range, with every kind of articulation of the bow. However, there has not, in general been a parallel advance in the making of stringed instruments. Developments in performing techniques have left the achievements of the violin-maker behind—or, putting it more harshly, the most accomplished violin-makers of the nineteenth century produced but little which compares favourably with the seventeenth- and eighteenth-century instruments of the Italians, and modern instruments too are rarely found to possess the tonal and visual qualities of the finest violins of that period. It is not a matter of age apparently, although it is clear that it takes a certain length of time—the period differs for different makers[1]—for an instrument to reach full maturity of tone. Probably, it has more to do with the training and experience gained by violin-makers, the time they could spend on each instrument, and the quality of the materials they worked with.

By now connoisseurs tend to dismiss as so much folk-lore the theory that the tone of the old Italian violins cannot be found again because the secret of the varnish used has been lost—obviously, they agree, the varnish had an important function, but it was one of many factors and was not the only one to have a strong influence on the tonal quality of the violin. The varnish can at best only bring out what is already inherent in the instrument, so that if it is the wrong shape, badly made or made of poor materials, the varnish won't improve on its shortcomings. On the other hand, the varnish could make its tone less attractive, if put on so that it clogged up the wood, were too heavy, too soft, or too hard. You might be interested to know that, although instrument makers polish, and even sometimes varnish the bore (the inside surface of the air column) of wind instruments, they do not polish, nor do they varnish the inside of a violin.

The perfect instrument is still very much an enigma, and although the measurements of some of the finest violins have been reproduced exactly, using the same assortment and quality of woods as in the original, the result, outstanding though it may be, is said to lack something.

What this is, is open to debate. While there is a great deal of systematized theory which the violin-maker has to know, his art relies as much on practical experience and on an intuitive response to the distinctive qualities of the materials in which he is working. Because of the particular honour in which the instrument is held in our culture, and, though we may be reluctant to admit it, because of the respect we have for an object that commands such an astronomical money value, a player's feelings about an old Italian violin are inevitably influenced by the knowledge that he may be handling one of the most highly admired instruments in existence.

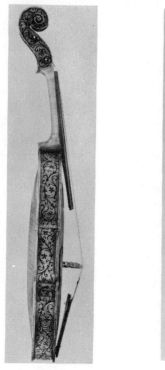  

Three views of an inlaid violin by Antonio Stradivarius 1683 Cremona (Hill Collection Ashmolena Museum Oxford)

[1] See p. 99.

The violin in Corelli's day was not exactly the same as the instrument with which we are familiar, although, unless you look carefully, you might think they looked much the same. In order to gain an impression of what the instrument Corelli played was like, let's check over the instrument as it is today, then note how the eighteenth-century violin differed from it.

Refer now to the diagram in *MI* 104 for the violin as we have it today.

The shape of the hollow sound-box of the violin varied from maker to maker, though only to a strictly limited extent. The violin might be narrow waisted, or fairly broad; highly arched over the front and back, or rather flat (though never completely so); it may have the appearance of being wide-shouldered, just as in another instrument your eye might be taken by the width and fullness of the lower part of the front. The proportions of the instrument could be varied but the volume inside the elegantly formed box is fairly constant. There is no standard shape to the violin, as you can see from such variations as I have mentioned, but as a guide its dimensions, if it is a 'full sized' violin, would be similar to these:

> Length of the back 14 inches
> Width $8\frac{1}{8}$ inches across the widest part of the bottom
> Width $6\frac{9}{16}$ inches across the 'shoulders'
> Sides $1\frac{1}{4}$ inches

The woods employed in the making of a violin are carefully chosen for their acoustical properties and have to be well seasoned before use. It is part of the violin-maker's craft to be able to recognize the potential of a piece of wood, even when it is still standing as a tree. It is possible, when looking at the instruments of the Italian masters (those which are so valuable that they are well documented), to see that many may have been made from the same good piece of wood: that there is a distinctive pattern in the grain of a spruce perhaps, which reappears in the fronts of a number of violins.

The front of a violin (also known as the table, belly, or top) is of a resilient softwood, spruce usually, while the head, neck, scroll, back and the ribs are made of maple or occasionally another hard wood. You will have noticed, on examining a violin, that the front may have a somewhat plain appearance, with the clear grain of the wood running the length of the instrument. But the hardwood of the back and head, particularly, are often striking, being chosen for their decorative as well as their acoustical properties. The four strings, tuned in fifths, run above a fingerboard of dark wood, ebony, which is very dense. The same wood is also used for the nut at the peg box end of the strings (see the diagram), the tailpiece, saddle and end pin, and the pegs, if not turned out of rosewood or boxwood, are of ebony too.

The strings pass over the bridge, delicately carved in maple, and are set in motion by the horsehair part of the bow. Many hardwoods are used for cheap bows, but for those of better quality a species of Brazilwood called Pernambuco is always used. The hair, naturally white horsehair for the best, otherwise bleached or made of nylon, is normally smooth, and needs to be covered in rosin to gain the necessary friction to set the strings vibrating. The rosin is itself another wood product, obtained by treating natural pine rosin with a number of ingredients. Violinists used to make their own rosin even in the last century, whereas now one buys a cake of rosin stuck to a cloth which enables one to rub the tightened horsehair of the bow into the rosin with one hand without getting the other hand sticky holding it.

Around the edges of the instrument, decoratively tracing the outline, is the purfling, three strips of dark, white and dark wood inlaid into both the table and the back. This has a protective function, to prevent splintering at the overhanging edges, or small chips and cracks spreading farther into the instrument. Inside, as may be seen from the diagram in *MI* page 109, are (softwood) side linings, again to add strength and, if you turn to the photographs of the inside of a violin and a double bass at plate 12, you will see how each of the corners is usually rounded off inside by a block. Then finally, two more parts of the violin which have, arguably, the most critical effect on the tone of the instrument if they are wrongly placed: the soundpost and the bass bar. So important is the soundpost that the French refer to it as 'the soul' of the instrument.

I have drawn attention briefly to a few points of the violin's construction. Read *MI* pages 102–31, the chapter on the violin by David D. Boyden.

Exercise

1 Suggest reasons for why the violin which is played today is not exactly the same as the instrument of Corelli's time.

2 Describe the main points of difference between the 'modern' violin and the eighteenth-century instrument.

My Comments

1 The distinction has mainly to do with weight and tension, as found in the violins themselves and in the manner of playing them. The alterations were brought about on account of changes in the musical environment, not the least influential of which was the shift from aristocratic, semi-private music making to the public concert which, in the nineteenth century, was accommodating more and more listeners. In an effort to ensure that large audiences should be able to hear the instruments involved, various things were done to the violin, as to other instruments, to make the production of a big sound possible, not always without the loss of attractive characteristics of tone and articulation.

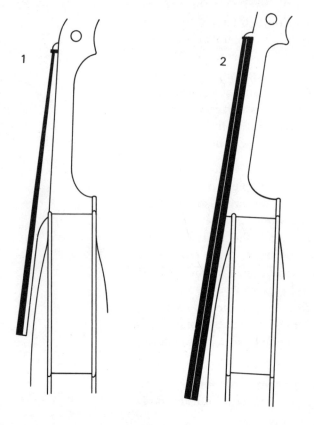

Neck of eighteenth-century violin and neck of modern violin (Die Musik in Geschichte und Gegenwart. Barenreiter)

2 To strengthen the belly of the 'modern' instrument, a heavier and, in most cases, slightly longer bass bar replaced the one already fitted. In an attempt to achieve a louder, more strident sound, the neck was increased slightly in length, and, so that it should be possible for the player to attack each string very heavily without sounding the neighbouring strings as well, the bridge was raised and its curvature increased. It was necessary to raise the fingerboard (which was lengthened as well for extended range) to follow the new angle of the strings—effectively done by tilting the whole of the neck back at an angle from the body.

Further Discussion

1 With regard to the demand for more volume and brilliance, for one thing, *pitch was raised*. Neither before the nineteenth century nor after (until very recently) was there uniformity of pitch throughout Europe. There were slight differences from one musical centre to another. But around about the beginning of the nineteenth century the pitch of all instruments rose by about a semitone, the rise in some musical centres being more, in others rather less. This meant that the open strings of the violin, for example, were tuned effectively a semitone higher.

It is unlikely that in itself this would have had much of a permanent effect on the tone of the violin. By screwing up the string to tune it up a semitone more pressure was being exerted on the bridge, the belly and the soundpost, etc. The resistance of the arching and the thickness of the wood in the belly and the back had been appropriate to the pressure before the rise in pitch. The soundpost had fitted exactly: not so tightly that it dampened the vibration of the plates (front and back) nor too loosely so that it failed to communicate the vibrations to the back and enabled the front and back to vibrate together. With the increase in pressure the soundpost would have been clamped in tightly between the belly and the back. The violin would have lost tone, so the musician would in all probability simply have asked a violin-maker to shorten the soundpost and put it back exactly where it used to be, or adjust its position so that it should not be held so tightly (by placing it a little nearer the middle of the violin. If you refer to the diagram of a cross-section of the body of a violin at the soundpost, in *MI* p. 109, you will notice that at the position in which the soundpost is placed the front and back are arching away from each other, thus making the change in the position of the soundpost described possible).

The instrument's former tone would probably have been restored—much depends on the instrument: a flatter model, such as a Stradivari, coming out of it better than the more highly arched violins of Amati and Stainer.

2 Very few violins, violas and cellos indeed escaped 'renovation' in the early nineteenth century, which means that hardly any pre-nineteenth-century instruments have their original bass bar, neck and fittings. If you have a chance to look at an eighteenth-century instrument or an earlier one, the neck of which does not come straight out of the body as shown in the first diagram above, you should be able to find a carefully made neck-graft at the foot of the head—but this is often so expertly done that it is almost impossible to detect it.

The modern violin, and by this I mean a violin *of any age* that is set up as I have just described, with the tilted neck, long fingerboard, long bass bar and so on, is appreciably heavier than the instrument played in the seventeenth and eighteenth centuries—mostly because of the ebony it carries. In the early violin the fingerboard was not only shorter, but also lighter, being made of a softwood such as spruce, and covered by the thinnest veneer of ebony. On the modern instrument this is solid ebony. In addition, the tail piece which is also now of

Antonio Stradivarius violin 'La Messie' 1716 (Hill Collection, Ashmolean Museum, Oxford)

ebony or another hardwood, used to be very lightly made of softwood. We now have a heavy hardwood chin-rest to the left of the tail piece, or if it is not shaped out of wood, it is moulded in vulcanite which is a little lighter. But in Corelli's time there was no need for a chin-rest at all since the violin was played with a much looser grip, with the instrument resting on the shoulder, the collarbone or even low on the breast, but not clenched up under the chin. Backing up the use of the chin-rest, most players now like using a shoulder rest, which according to its design may or may not inadvertently dampen the vibration of the back (which is less than that of the front anyway). It is added weight to the violin. The strings are of different materials as well, of course, although this would not have an effect on the weight of the violin.

3 To the points noted here must be added changes in the development of the bow (see *MI* 116 ff.) which also affected the tonal properties of the violin. These are audible when one has the opportunity to hear a comparison of different bows on modern as well as 'old' instruments. Of greater importance, however, was the effect the character of the bow had on the way the player performed the music. There were in the eighteenth century a variety of bows in use for the violin. In any given musical centre one is unlikely to have found *all* the types referred to, since most of the musicians occupied in making music in one place were likely to be using the same kind of bows in the same music. But in England, knowing the reluctance with which musicians here eventually gave up instruments of the viol family, it is certainly possible, if not probable, that viol bows would also have been seen in the ensemble.

The old kinds of violin bow and the viol bow, being deeper between the stick and the hair, had more 'give' in them than the modern bow. Whether one wishes it or not, this imposes a characteristic kind of articulation[1] on the music

---

[1] By *articulation* is meant the way, in particular, that the notes are started (gently or sharply) and ended (cut off dead or allowed to run into the next note).

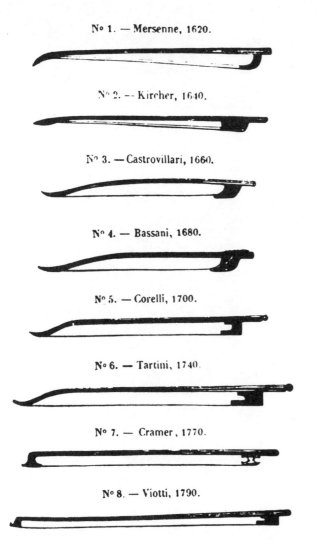

Nº 1. — Mersenne, 1620.

Nº 2. -- Kircher, 1640.

Nº 3. — Castrovillari, 1660.

Nº 4. — Bassani, 1680.

Nº 5. — Corelli, 1700.

Nº 6. — Tartini, 1740.

Nº 7. — Cramer, 1770.

Nº 8. — Viotti, 1790.

A sequence of bows purporting to represent the development of the bow from Mersenne to Viotti (from D. Boyden, The History of Violin Playing, OUP)

(*MI* 123–4). If it is borne in mind that eighteenth-century bows were *not* the same as the kind of bow we use now, that they had a particular character which suited the music written at that time ideally, it becomes less likely that inappropriate tempi and kinds of articulation are chosen in performances today of eighteenth-century music.

Tempi were all rather slower in the days of Corelli and Vivaldi than they are in general now. That the bow had a decisive influence on the tempo at which the music went, should go without saying. And having observed that it was a characteristic of the early eighteenth-century bow that it imposed a somewhat slower but a more deliberate and distinct kind of articulation than the modern bow, it should not be difficult to see for example, an Allegro movement from a Baroque sonata or concerto, not as a hectic dash from beginning to end, but as music in which all the phrases or passages of pattern work need to be played more slowly and distinctly if they are to count at all. The horse-hair of a bow does not last indefinitely; it becomes too smooth to act efficiently as a means of setting the vibrations in the strings in motion. How long it goes without needing to be re-haired depends on various factors—first of all the player, the amount of use it gets, the kind of music played, temperature, humidity—but even if a bow is re-haired very often, and if too much hair is put on to it, or too little, it does not alter the underlying character of the bow. The important thing is its form, the balance and weight, and the amount of spring in it.

Exercise

Identify the parts numbered on this sketch of an eighteenth-century violin.

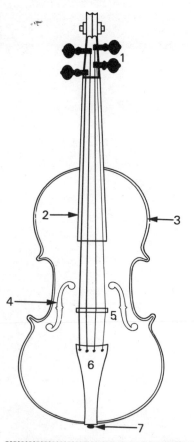

Answer

1 peg box and scroll
2 short finger-board
3 purfling
4 f hole

5 bridge
6 tailpiece
7 end pin and saddle

Note in particular the short finger-board, and the absence of a chin rest to the left of the tailpiece.

In the seventeenth and early eighteenth centuries the violin bow was commonly held either by the 'French' grip (which was not only used in France, however) or the 'Italian'.

Of these the thumb-under-hair 'French' grip afforded firmness without much subtlety or nuance, it gave the player a direct contact with the bow hair (as in viol playing) and, above all, it was very effective for a straight-forward rhythmic and articulated bow stroke needed in dance music. In spite of its name (probably applied later), this bow grip was not limited to the French at this time, being widespread in Italy and elsewhere. The other basic grip was later called the 'Italian' grip, the thumb being placed between the hair and bow stick. This grip was better suited to the more varied and subtle strokes of the advanced Italian technique, especially of the sonata players. The French grip probably became obsolete in Italy before the end of the seventeenth century, but it prevailed in France until the Italian sonata gained a firm foothold there about 1725. In both these grips, the arm, elbow, and wrist were apparently held freely and loosely. The resulting stroke must normally have been a light and articulated one, rather than powerful and heavy. Nevertheless, the ideal stroke was played well into the string. . . . The position of the fingers with respect to the frog (nut) is dependent on the length of the bow and its balance. With the

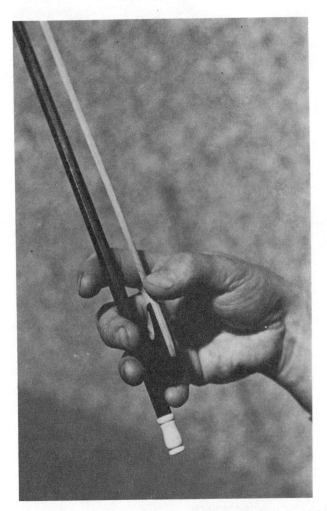
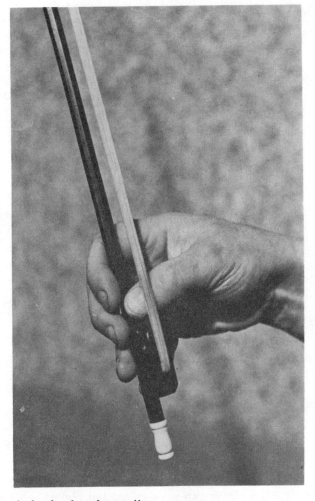

short bow, which generally prevailed in this period, the hand usually gripped the bow at the frog itself. In the eighteenth century, particularly with longer bows, a typical grip was several inches above the frog. The volume of sound was presumably controlled by pressure from the first finger, which usually gripped the stick at the first joint.[1]

Two bow grips, thumb on and thumb under

With regard to the grip on the bow in the period in which the 'French' grip was going out of use in favour of the more controlled grip preferred by the Italians, here is a passage from an early eighteenth-century music book in which the author remarks on the playing of the Italian virtuoso Nicola Matteis. He came to settle in England in the early 1670s, a time when music in this country was very strongly influenced by what went on in France, and clearly the 'French' grip was the one used by English musicians.

> His manner of using his violin was much out of the comon road of handling, but out of it he made the utmost of sound, double, single, swift, and all manners of touch, which made such impressions that his audience was not onely pleased but full of wonder at him, and his way of performing. He was a very tall and large bodyed man, used a very long bow, rested his instrument against his short ribbs, and with that (having onely a full accompaniment) could hold an audience by the ears longer than ordinary, and a whisper not be heard amongst them. In short the character of that man, to those who never saw or heard him, is incredible; but out of that awkwardness he taught the English to hold the bow by the wood onely and not to touch the hair, which was no small reformation.[2]

[1] *HVP*, 152–3.

[2] *NOM*, 309.

Exercise

What are the points North considered worth commenting upon, in the manner in which Matteis played? His virtuosity and ability to present a piece well must have been very considerable, but what else?

My Comments

North mentions also:

1 That his bow was longer than customary in England (the Italian sonata bow was, indeed, longer than the bow favoured by the French and English for playing dance music); 2 he held his violin up against *the bottom of his ribs*, which, on this very tall man must have looked incredibly awkward and low to English players. Typical positions for playing the violin are described in *MI*, pp. 115, 118, 122, as also subsequently in this unit; 3 that he did not touch the hair of the bow with his fingers, as in the 'French' grip; 4 that he had a most attractive style of embellishing his music; 5 that he led English taste in favour of Italian music.

The second observation made by North on Matteis's playing, the lower position of holding the violin, is worth remarking on. In the seventeenth and eighteenth centuries the violin was played in concert music in a variety of positions, all exhibiting a fairly relaxed grip, and by no means exclusively with the violin held under the chin. To most of us today a violin played in any position other than under the chin may seem unusual, and we may suppose all other positions less efficient and more difficult to cope with. Positions in which the violin is held against the body *are* less efficient for playing difficult music involving rapid changes in position of the left hand. But it is to a great extent a matter of what the player can get used to, and remarkable things are sometimes demonstrated to be possible. There is a very substantial folk tradition of violin playing in which the instrument is not held as for conventional concert music. You can see Norwegian, Polish, Hungarian and other folk musicians today playing with

Beethoven's quartet instruments presented by Prince Carl Lichnovsky 1800. Left to right, viola by Rugero 1690, cello by A. Guarnerius 1675, unknown viola, violin by N. Amati 1690, violin by G. Guarnerius 1718 (Collection Dr H. C. Bodmer, Beethoven-Haus, Bonn)

82

the violin held lower than the shoulder—against the collarbone or on the breast. As an example of this way of holding the violin here is a photograph of a Norwegian folk musician.[1] Compare it with the violin grip of the seventeenth-century French dancing master in the painting by Gerard Dou (1665). The question of whether the violin should be held under the chin or loosely propped up against the body does not really become an important one where dance music is concerned. It is not usual for dance music to require a great range, and the player may be able to accompany a whole dance without moving his left hand up or down the fingerboard of his violin. His hand remains in the same *position* although he moves his fingers very actively.

> 'Position' is a technical term in string playing: in string playing, the 'position' of the left hand higher or lower on the fingerboard. In the first (or natural) position, the first finger stops a whole tone above the open string. In the higher positions, the first finger stops the correspondingly higher notes of the diatonic scale. Thus in third position the first finger stops a fourth above the open string.[2]

By changing position the violinist is changing gear, as it were: with each 'shift' up he gains a higher range while losing his lowest notes until he shifts back to the first position. It is easy, when the violin is held under the chin, to move the hand up and down to any position, because the violin is supported by the chin and shoulder. Its weight is not being taken by the left hand. However, with the violin propped up against the player's breast or collarbone, the playing hand is actually holding the violin up, so although it is easy enough to shift the hand into higher and higher positions, the problem comes when the first position is wanted again. The player has to release his grip on the neck of the violin and extend his arm away from the body. It may only be a matter of two or three inches, but while he is sliding his hand this distance along the neck, his violin is not securely supported. The French violinist in the painting by Dou would probably support it with his wrist, but the Angel would be in danger of dropping his fiddle.

In the nineteenth century, violinists added a chin rest and then shoulder support to hold the violin up. The additions encouraged a tense, 'death grip' hold of the violin under the chin, and recklessness of the left hand; both are bad faults inherent in modern playing technique.

I have isolated here two points of importance in violin technique: the manner of holding the instrument with the left hand, and the grip on the bow with the right. People who have not learned to play an instrument of the violin family often overlook the basic fact that good playing requires not only an ability to reach all the notes and to finger them in tune, but also a good bowing technique. The bow draws the sound from an instrument, and the way it is handled can endow the sound with a wide range of nuances. That this was so was shown during the Baroque period most noticeably in music written in variation form. The Paduan virtuoso violinist Giuseppe Tartini (1692–1770) actually entitled a set of fifty variations which he composed on a theme of Corelli 'The Art of Bowing' (*L'Arte del Arco*). The variation was frequently treated in Baroque music as an exposition of different kinds of bowing. Examples of such pieces you might look out for are the Tartini variations mentioned, from which we have an excerpt on Baroque Music II, and the chaconne from the *Partita in D minor for unaccompanied violin* by J. S. Bach. You have an opportunity to hear and see a performance of this partita in the fourth television programme.

[1] The leading player of his generation, T. Augundsson, known as 'Myllarguten', who died in 1872. This position is still commonly used.

[2] *HVP*, 527.

Angel playing the Renaissance fiddle. Detail from altarpiece by Hans Memling c. 1500 (Anvers; Photo Mansell Collection)

Torgeir Augundsson of Telemark, 1801–72, the famous Norwegian 'Myllarguten' (Norske Folkemuseum)

Violinist playing in the French style, a lithograph of a painting by Gerard Dou 1665 (Dresden Gemaldegalerie; Photo Mansell Collection)

One of the principles in the discipline of bowing which exercised theorists and players alike during the seventeenth and early eighteenth centuries was the one which came to be known as the 'Rule of the Down-Bow'. This derives from the fact that in violin playing, the down-bow is naturally weighted while the up-bow is not. The down-bow consequently came to be related to stressed beats (for example, the first beat of a bar) and the up-bow to beats or the parts of a beat which are unstressed. There are of course complications, as you can gather from these instructions given by the Frenchman Marin Mersenne (1636), but the rule was generally followed at the time, and it ought therefore to be borne in mind in performing Baroque music today.

> One ought always to draw the bow downward on the first note of the measure and the bow must be pushed up on the following note . . . the bow is always drawn downward on the first note of each measure composed of an even number of notes, but if a measure is composed of an unequal number . . . one draws the bow upward on the first note of the following measure so as to draw it down again on the first note of the third measure.[1]

The range called for in Baroque music gradually extended from the bottom open G string to a''' which is the seventh position on the E string,

This is the working range used in the violin treatises of Leopold Mozart and Geminiani in the mid-eighteenth century. Exceptionally, however, Pietro Locatelli (1695–1764) takes the violin up to the fourteenth position in the *caprices*, of Concerto XI of his *L'Arte del Violino* (1733). These *caprices* are cadenzas of a technical difficulty unsurpassed until by Paganini a century later. Although the higher positions were naturally used on the top string to extend the upper range of the violin, they were also called for in passages of multiple stopping or arpeggios for the three lower strings. When a composer intended a particular tone colour to be carried through a melody and indicated that it was all to be played on one string, higher positions might be used then too.

4.2 The Viola

Much of what has been said on the violin applies to the other instruments of the family, particularly in the matter of developments in the construction and fitting up of the instruments. The instruments were lightly constructed up to the beginning of the nineteenth century then, being more substantially reinforced, heavier fittings were used in the period in which a bigger, more strident sound was called for.

The appearance and playing technique of the viola is very similar to that of the violin, but the tone of a viola seldom has the lightness of a violin, a characteristic which Romantic composers were not slow to take advantage of in 'dark' passages.

The viola, however, was not an instrument which received much sympathetic attention in the Baroque period, as you will see in reading the following passages.

[1] *HVP*, 158.

Exercise

Read the section on the viola written by Kenneth Skeaping, in *MI*. Take note in particular of pages 132–4, and jot down the three most important points of difference mentioned between the viola and the violin.

My Answer

1 The viola was less standardized in size than the violin. The sizes most commonly found were the large instrument with a body length of up to $18\frac{1}{2}$ inches, and the smaller-sized of around about 15 inches—only an inch longer than a violin, in other words.

2 Although both violin and viola were members of the new family which ousted the viols, the viola came off badly because of the style of the music which was then being written.

3 The viola was neglected. When used at all it was treated cautiously, and consequently it attracted the poorest players.

Further Comment

The relationship between the viola itself and the music written for it is one of those very odd chicken-and-the-egg cases. The viola came into existence at the beginning of the period when the violin was competing with the viols for attention. It is still open to debate whether, in fact, it preceded the violin or not. But having come into the hands of musicians just at the time when the more adventurous of them were taking up the violin, it made little impact. It was overshadowed by its more brilliant relation. There was less contrast between the tone of a viola and that of a tenor viol, for example, than between that of the violin and of the treble viol.

In its early days the violin began to make headway through playing for dancing. The viola's lower compass did not suit it so well for this activity in a solo role, although violas predominated in the French court orchestra whose main function was playing dance music. But of greater significance was the harmonic consequences of the change in style at the beginning of the seventeenth century. Whereas a viola player might perfectly adequately have taken a part in consort music, as you see in the second television programme of the course, when used in a group playing music in the new Baroque style it found itself belonging more obviously to the continuo section—or, as Kenneth Skeaping puts it in his chapter in *MI*, it was put 'to scrape the harmonic leavings of the other parts'.

As you know from our discussion of the continuo, the emphasis in the Baroque style was on the bass line itself, the harmonic progression, and the melodies at the top derived from the progression. The viola was very seldom given the opportunity to contribute a melody 'at the top', and since composers had that very useful kind of musical shorthand, the figured bass, for indicating the harmony intended above the bass line, they frequently did not note the middle parts of the texture at all; and so the viola was regarded as very much a drudge instrument.

The forms of music which composers found most attractive and challenging from the mid-seventeenth to the mid-eighteenth centuries were the sonata—in particular for one instrument with continuo, and for two equally important melody instruments and continuo, the trio sonata—and the large-scale forms of these, the solo concerto and concerto grosso. The trio sonata omitted the viola completely, seeing it as too low in pitch to take one of the top-line parts and too high to act as a bass line instrument. As for its use in concertos, as a solo instrument, it was only considered by composers as prolific as Vivaldi and Telemann, who wrote concertos for so many different combinations of instruments that the viola was almost bound to be included sooner or later. But these were exceptional, and if there were any aspiring viola players in the period they were given little encouragement by the parts written for them as ripieno players in the orchestra.

Although Vivaldi frequently writes two ripieno viola parts in his concertos most other composers failed to see what an attractive instrument the viola was, and the viola player could count himself lucky if he even had an independent line at all.[1] In a great deal of music the viola simply doubles the bass part at the octave above, joining thus the continuo section which may already consist of one or two keyboard instruments, cellos, violas da gamba, double bass, and a bassoon or two. Handel was no exception in this matter, although obviously it was not because he couldn't write the extra part in counterpoint. There are many movements in his *Six Concertos, op. 3* in which the viola has this kind of part. Not infrequently, when the bass part rises and the melody falls fairly low so that the harmony is closely spaced, the viola protrudes through the upper part, destroying the line and creating an odd if not unpleasant effect harmonically. But in such cases the composer left it to the viola player to adapt the part, by dropping an octave, or missing it out altogether. Such viola parts continued to be written even in the late-eighteenth century in, for example, some of Haydn's symphonies.

It was a vicious circle, as Adam Carse has pointed out in his book *The Orchestra in the XVIIIth Century* (p. 143).

> composers wrote poor parts for the viola because the instrument was not well played, and it was not well played because composers wrote such poor parts for it.

Carse translates a passage from the famous treatise on playing the flute by Quantz (1752), in which the author admitted that the viola was looked upon as an inferior instrument:

> The viola is commonly regarded as a thing of little consequence in music. This may be because the instrument is generally played either by beginners or by those who have no particular talent for playing the violin, or perhaps it is unprofitable to the player; therefore, able musicians are not at all anxious to play it.

But Charles Avison, in his *An Essay on Musical Expression* (1752), insisted that for the performance of any instrumental music,

> In the four principal Parts there ought to be four Performers of almost equal Mastery . . .

---

[1] We might compare the independent viola part to the occasional 4′ pedal melody in German organ music, as mentioned in unit 2 for example.

However, on reflection he conceded that

> this Rule is generally neglected by placing one of the worst Hands to the *Tenor*; which, though a Part of little execution, yet requires so much Meaning and Expression, that the Performer should not only give a fine Tone, (the peculiar Quality of that Instrument) but by swelling and singing of the Notes, and entering into the Spirit of the Composer, know, without destroying the *Air*, where to fill the *Harmony*; and, by boldly pointing the Subject, keep it up with the greatest Energy.

Hawkins[1] has a nice line on a good violinist who took to playing the viola.

> About the year 1750 Barsanti returned to England ... being advanced in years, he was glad to be taken into the opera band as a performer on the tenor violin.

The viola continued to be neglected by composers after the *galant* style had been established in England, and in all probability the shortage of good viola players continued too, although the situation would not seem to have been desperate in London if the list of players taking part in the great Handel Commemoration is anything to go by. Amongst the instrumentalists privileged to perform in the 1784 celebrations were twenty-six viola players, a modest figure alongside the ninety-five violinists but evidence that there were at least twenty-six men who could play the viola!

It was as a result of the viola's neglect, and after failing to find a single solo for it in the music shops of London that William Flackton decided to write some himself, and in 1770 published his *Six Solo's Three for a Violoncello, and Three for a Tenor*. The publication bears the mark of Flackton's two professions, those of musician and bookseller. That he was 'in the trade' is shown by the contacts he had in London, for the solos were 'Printed for the Author and Sold by him in Canterbury, C. & S. Thompson, Mr. Randall, Mrs. Johnson, Mr. Longman, Mr. Bremner, Mr. Welcker . . .' The list of places at which the pieces could be purchased includes all the leading music shops in the city. But although he kept a bookshop for over half a century, Flackton was also a well known viola player and teacher. It is to be regretted that he wrote no concertos for his favourite instrument for it is clear from the Preface to his solos that he really felt for the instrument, and was by no means a disappointed violinist who had 'escaped' to the viola. The first part of the Preface which follows may be taken as an honest reflection on the status and employment of the instrument at that time.

> The Solos for a Tenor Violin are intended to show that Instrument in a more conspicuous Manner, than it has hitherto been accustomed; the Part generally allotted to it being little more than a dull Ripiano, an Accessory or Auxiliary, to fill up or compleat the Harmony in Full Pieces of Music; though it must be allowed, that at some particular Times, it has been permitted to accompany a Song, and likewise to lead in a Fugue yet even then it is assisted by one, or more Instruments in the Unison or Octaves, to prevent, if possible its being distinguished from any other Instrument; or, if it happens to be heard but in so small a Space as a Bar or two, 'tis quickly overpowered again with a Crowd of Instruments, and lost in Chorus.

[1] *HH*, ii, 896.

Two positions for playing the viola

Such is the Present State of this Fine Toned Instrument, owing in some Measure, to the Want of Solos, and other Pieces of Music, properly adapted to it. . . .

It does sound as if things were tough for the viola, and Felton's description of it overpowered by a crowd of instruments is quite a tear-jerker. But not all composers were insensitive to its tone, nor without interest in improving its lot. After all, to release the viola from a position of secondary importance would mean to gain another active and responsible member of the orchestra. As long as the music being composed was in the Baroque style, however, little headway was to be made. We shall be seeing later how it was not until the music of Haydn (the later string quartets particularly), Mozart and Beethoven that the potential of the viola to contribute anything more than a thematically insignificant element of the texture was realised. If you read the Arts Second Level *Age of Revolutions* Course, you may recall that in the *Beethoven* units I wrote how Beethoven's handling of the viola, giving it a part of greater responsibility so that the more important thematic material was fairly 'democratically' shared between the four members of the string quartet, was a distinctive personal characteristic of his music, just as it contributed very much to the emancipation of the viola. But Baroque composers were encumbered in their use of this instrument by the fact that, even assuming there was one available, which was not always, it was unlikely to be played with any degree of skill.

An interesting attempt at a solution was made by Geminiani in his set of concertos op. 3. These were published in London in 1733 with the title *Concerti grossi con Due Violini Viola e Violoncello di Concerti Obligati e Due altri Violini e Basso di Concerto Grosso*. (Grand Concertos for a solo group consisting of two violins, viola and cello with two other violin parts and a bass for the ripieno.) The unusual feature of these concertos is in the scoring of the parts. Was it perhaps his attempt to improve the standard of viola playing? He raised the status of the viola by transferring it from the ripieno into the solo group, leaving the ripieno without the middle part. It was no loss, rather, a realistic admission of the viola's ineffective role in the accompaniment. Twenty-two years later, encouraged possibly by the reception the op. 3 concertos had received (from viola players especially), Geminiani issued the concertos in score—a most unusual thing to do in those days. They were thoroughly revised and, continuing his trend in favour of the viola, a *Viola di Ripieno* part was added and the concertino viola's part was made more active. But the idea was not taken up at the time by the English musicians who would have played them. Only after the Baroque style had been superseded in England do we find someone using the viola in a way which resembles in this particular that of Geminiani. Charles Wesley (not the Rev. Charles Wesley, hymn-writer and brother of John Wesley the founder of Methodism, but his son) published in *c.* 1782 his *Concerto Grosso*, a piece which harks back nostalgically to the 'Antient Style'. Like Geminiani, Wesley has a viola in the solo group but, since he takes the keyboard instrument out of it to play only with the ripieno, the solo group he exposes is the modern string quartet.

The viola da gamba (Weigel, J. C. Musicalisches Theatrum. courtesy Barenreiter)

A final indication of the rate at which the viola 'emerged' may be seen in the following two related actions. In about 1810 that ever-active musical amateur John Marsh, the man with the organ in his house playable from two rooms (section 2.4), seeing the need for a tutorbook for the viola, wrote one entitled *Instructions and progressive lessons for the tenor*. Some seventy years later, notwithstanding an immense corpus of Romantic music (including Berlioz's *Harold in Italy* for viola and orchestra), this same tutorbook was brought out again under its original title by a well-known publishing house in London. If the viola was not still to some extent neglected in comparison with the violin, how otherwise would this tutorbook couched in typically Georgian language, with the viola called a tenor, and symphonies described as 'modern full pieces', have been countenanced in Victorian England?

A close relative of the viola is the viola d'amore. It is sometimes heard in concertos by Vivaldi. This rare and intriguing-looking instrument, with its set of sympathetic strings passing through the bridge, is something of a cross between instruments of the viol and of the violin families. Tonally it has closer affinities to the viola than any other instrument.

There is a short account of it in *MI* p. 189, with a photograph at Plate 18, to which you might turn now.

You know already the opening Adagio of Ariosti's *Lesson in A major* for viola d'amore, on Baroque music II side 2 band 7, from the recording of which you have a fair impression of the instrument's agility and expressive quality of tone.

Play Baroque Music II side 2 band 7

Mozart and Beethoven were particularly influential in freeing the viola from its former subservient and rather useless position. The fact that they both *liked playing the viola*, and obviously knew what it could do, counted a lot. Johann Sebastian Bach was also fond of playing the viola when he was not either at the harpsichord or, as Konzertmeister, taking a solo violin part. In the last of the set of *Brandenburg Concertos* he dispenses with violins altogether and writes two solo parts for violas which are the most gratifying in the whole of Baroque music. You have an opportunity of getting to know a movement from this concerto well, and looking closely at Bach's use of the instruments in units 7-9. To hear the viola at its most active, listen now to the finale of the *Sixth Brandenburg Concerto*.

Play Baroque Music III side 2 band 6

4.3   Bass Instruments: the violoncello, viola da gamba, double bass and violone

The cello fared comparatively well in the eighteenth century, and there are quite a number of rewarding solos and duets, as well as concertos for it. But like the viola da gamba, double bass and violone its main function was to contribute to the basso continuo, as you already know. Unlike the violin, the cello did not succeed in captivating musicians to such an extent that it was taken up early during the Baroque period in preference to its corresponding member of the viol family. For one thing it was competing with what was tonally the most attractive size of viol, the viola da gamba, which cultured musical amateurs had for a century been handling and playing with obvious satisfaction. The viola da gamba ('*leg* viol') incidentally, is a very misleading name, since all the viols except the very largest, are played supported between the knees.

*Frederick, Prince of Wales
and his sisters, by P. Mercier
1707–1751* (National
Portrait Gallery)

*Marie Louise playing the
bass viol, by Nattier* (Musee
de Versailles; Mansell
Collection)

Exercise

To remind you of the distinctive tone of a viola da gamba, listen now to the following pieces: the first two with viola da gamba and the other two using cello. How would you describe the tonal difference between the cello and the viola da gamba?

viola da gamba: Rameau *Pièces de clavecin* 'La Livri'; J. S. Bach, Trio sonata from *The Musical Offering*, Allegro.

Play Baroque Music II side 1 band 6 and band 4

cello: Leclair *Sonata op. 5 no. 6* 'Le Tombeau', Grave; J. S. Bach *Suite no. 3 for cello* Allemande

Play Baroque Music II side 2 bands 5 and 6

My Comments

The cello's tone is both fuller and heavier than that of the viola da gamba, a quality which was not at that time seen as particularly advantageous by musicians whose idea of beauty was very much concerned with clarity and lightness. This was why the gamba was more commonly used in France and England, where the old-style music continued to be played longer than in Germany and, in particular, Italy. In Italy, the home of the sonata, the cello quickly established itself in the seventeenth century as the equal if not immediately the superior of the gamba for playing continuo—something the cello did not succeed in doing in France and England for almost a century. Corelli, incidentally, was amongst those who preferred the cello for continuo playing to the gamba or violone.

The tone of the gamba has the effect of making the instrument sound an octave higher than it is. In the Rameau you may have felt this particularly. Its responsiveness and agility certainly contributed to its popularity for playing *divisions*, or virtuoso variations on a ground bass.

Further Comment

The cello and gamba were both used in seventeenth- and eighteenth-century music as and when available, although, the cello was taking the place of the gamba more and more in Germany and Italy from the late seventeenth century. In the case of the upper viols, however, their 'passing out' happened more decisively. You will hear for yourself in the second television programme a treble viol and a violin play two of the upper parts in a piece by John Dowland. The treble viol tone, nasal in quality, may not to seventeenth-century ears have sounded mean in comparison with the violin's, but there certainly was something about the *character* of the latter and the music to which it seemed so ideally suited which musicians found more appealing than the treble viol. As John Playford writes in 1666,[1] 'The *Treble Violin* is a cheerful and spritely Instrument, and much practised of late. . . .'

My comments on the violin and viola, relating to their construction, again apply largely to the cello. But for a detailed description of the instrument and of its rise to prominence read now the chapter on the cello in *MI*, pages 137–49.

[1] *A Brief Introduction to the Skill of Musick*, 89.

Turn to the score of the Allemande from J. S. Bach *Suite No. 3*, which is in unit 10.

The opening flourish establishes the key of C major, with a figure extending over two octaves right down to bottom C, the cello's lowest string. That the cello is tuned in fifths may be seen from Bach's idiomatic writing for the instrument. The two lower strings are tuned to C and G. Note how these are used in turn (bars 6 and 7) as pedals, above which other parts move in double stopping. The range used in this movement is two and a half octaves—up to g' in bars 7–9. In normal continuo playing the upper and lower extremes were infrequently used.

Listen to this movement now while following the score. You should note that, like the violin, the cello is capable of playing lightly with agility (there are wide leaps in bars 7 and 11, for example), of playing chords (bars 5 and 6); and of articulating with a variety of bowings (of which only a few are here).

Play Baroque Music II side 2 band 6

In the eighteenth century, the cello was played without the supporting spike at the base. It was gripped between the player's knees like the viola da gamba. Look out for this on the second television programme of the course.

But to consider the construction of the viol, and the difference in between the way it and the cello are played, read now the short chapter 'The Viols' by Thurston Dart in *MI* pages 184–90.

Apart from getting the historical perspective right, you should have noted in these two accounts a number of points relating to the other instruments in the viol and violin families as well.

The matter of size and proportion is a fascinating one: the proportions of the viol remain fairly constant from the treble to the viola da gamba (*MI*, page 187). But the cello, while similar to the violin from the front is seen to be proportionally much deeper when viewed from the side. Details of this are given in *MI*, page 137.

Another important difference to be noted emerges in the right-hand technique of playing instruments of the violin and viol families: the grip on the bow.

In playing a viol the bow is held with the palm of the hand outward and with the second and third finger actually on the hair. Imagine you are going to shake hands with someone who is standing in front of you a little to your right: you are extending your bow hand to him. If you now bend your wrist back and allow your fingers to close inward as is most comfortable, this position resembles that of the grip on the viol bow and it is also a grip used by some double bass players. In playing the violin, viola, cello and, for some players the double bass, instead of the palm of the hand being in that position on the same side as the hair of the bow, it is *above* the stick facing downwards. And, to make a very rough comparison (if we were not using the 'French' grip described earlier) the stick is held with the fingers gripping it loosely in a position similar to the grip you would use if you had picked up a pen and were about to put it into your breast pocket.

Johan Schenck with viola da gamba—mezzotint by Peter Schenck (Royal College of Music)

If you are unfamiliar with the bow grips I am describing, make a special point of looking out for them in the second television programme of the course, in which we introduce the stringed instruments of the period.

Exercise

Read the chapter on the double bass in *MI* (pages 149–56) and jot down your answers to these questions:

1 Like the viola, the double bass was an instrument which had no accepted standard size. It had, moreover, no standard shape. Describe the various forms of the double bass.

2 Give the various tunings and number of strings of the double bass.

3 How does the double bass differ from the violone, the largest·of the viols? The two instruments, though used in the same way in ensemble music, were not synonymous.

62

The violone (left) and the double bass

My Comments

1 Most basses stand over six feet high, with the body some forty-four inches long. The true double bass violin, with swelled back and the shape of the violin, is not common because it is more awkward to play than the form of double bass which bears resemblance to the viol. This has sloping shoulders and a flat back, the depth of the back is reduced at the shoulders so that the player can play more conveniently further down the finger-board. The flat back is thus angled in towards the neck at the shoulder.

2 The double bass most commonly used has four strings tuned, not in fifths as other members of the violin family are, but in fourths: E.A.d.g. The three-string bass is tuned to G.d.g. or A.d.g. Basses with five strings may be tuned like a four-string bass with the addition of a low C string a third below the open E, or alternatively in fourths up from E—so that the fifth string is an addition above, rather than below the more usual set of four strings. Six-string basses were apparently common in the eighteenth century. They are not seen in orchestras today.

3 The double bass has the characteristic f-shaped sound holes and pointed corners of instruments of the violin family. The violone has the rounded corners of a viol, and either C-shaped or flame-shaped sound holes like the other viols, it is also fretted (with gut frets tied round the neck and finger-board) whereas the double bass is not. Usually the double bass has four strings, the violine has six; the violone's tone is lighter than that of the double bass.

Further Discussion

The double bass and violone used to be referred to in Victorian treatises on instrumentation as the 'sixteen foot' of the orchestra. This you ought to recognize, having read unit 1, as a piece of organists' terminology for pedal stops which sound an octave lower than written. You will remember that the term '8 ft. pitch' derives from the fact that the speaking length of the pipe which provides the bottom note of an organ manual keyboard C is about 8 feet.

The organist knew that if he played a piece with the simplest registration of a single 8′ stop he would hear the music at the pitch it was notated: pressing the middle C key, he would hear the note middle C. If he added a 16′ stop, he would also hear the note an octave lower (unit 1 section 2.3), but he would rarely have a use for the 16′ stop on its own without the 8′ to sound the music at the pitch it was notated.

The double bass and the violone were used in ensemble music, when they were available, to add depth to the continuo, doubling the cello and viola da gamba, or whatever was playing the notated bass line, an octave lower. They would seldom be used alone. Because the players read the same part as the cello or gamba but the sound which came out was *not* actually what was written, but an octave lower, these are known as *transposing instruments*.

To have written out a double bass part at the pitch intended would have meant using a great number of ledger lines under the bass stave, which in printed music adds greatly to the expense. In the seventeenth and eighteenth centuries musicians were notoriously practically minded: they were perfectly aware of the conventions all musicians practised, so they did not bother or need to indicate in writing details they could take for granted. A double bass is a very large and cumbersome instrument. There were relatively few of them around. Although a composer knew his music would sound better with the bass line reinforced by a double bass he also faced the fact that there was no certainty at all that a player of this instrument would be on hand for every performance of his piece. He wrote his music, therefore, in such a way that it would work without one. Generally, the double bass and the violone, if either was available, would join in on the Basso Ripieno line, which never has an indispensable solo part.

Despite their size, these two instruments can be played with great agility by a virtuoso performer. Examples of such writing are the double bass concerto in E by Dittersdorf, and the concerto for violone by Capuzzi, which you may have heard. In general, however, judging by the comments of eighteenth-century writers, the standard of the average double bass player committed him to the ranks of the 'gentlemen' rather than the 'players' and even then he had to learn certain dodges which enabled him not to get left behind by the rest of the orchestra.

It was the viola problem all over again ('putting the worst Hand to the Tenor'). Quantz observed that players of the double bass were the musicians who did not have enough ability to play any other instrument properly. Not only did they play so badly out of tune that he suggested they should tie gut frets around the neck and finger-board as on the violone, but because they habitually fell so badly out of time they were enjoined to simplify their parts in rapid passages by missing out alternate notes, or to take a selection of notes which they could play in tempo from the given part.[1]

[1] Adam Carse, *The Orchestra in the XVIIIth Century*, 123.

The Lute

The lute was already highly admired before the Baroque style became current and, although some music was written for it during the Baroque era its history, at this time, like that of the viols was one of decline.

The lute is a plucked instrument, fretted, and capable of playing both chords and expressive melodies. In Baroque music its chief function was playing continuo parts, so it was its capacity as a chord-playing instrument which was mainly called for. As lutenists were not accustomed to playing from music notation, however, but from a distinctive kind of tablature in which the notes to be played are indicated by letters or numerals, they were barred from participating easily in ensemble music. There is a short account of the lute and kindred instruments, in *MI* pages 157–65, which is informative.

You will have an opportunity of seeing both the lute and the chittarone— which is such an impressive instrument on account of its size, and the large number of strings it has—in the second television programme. Although the harpsichord was the 'chord-playing' instrument most commonly used for the continuo in the Baroque period, Corelli actually specifies on the title page of his op. 1 trio sonatas that an archlute might be used. This is why the chittarone, a form of archlute, is used to play a movement from the first of the op. 1 sonatas in this programme.

A point which might have raised your curiosity in reading these accounts of stringed instruments and one which keeps on coming up in most discussions of musical instruments, is the matter of *age* and the advantages it brings tonally to an instrument.

Touching on the point, Thomas Mace, an English musician who was an authority on the viol and lute, drew this conclusion as to the advantages age endows upon an instrument:

Lute player

At first, it is a newly made instrument; and therefore cannot yet speak as well as it will do, when it comes to age and ripeness; yet it gives forth a very free, brisk, trouling, plump and sweet sound: but it is generally known, that age adds goodness and perfection to all instruments made of wood; therefore old lutes and viols are always of much more value than new ones; so that if an instrument be good, when new, there is no doubt but it will be excellent, when it is old. . . . The reasons for which, I can no further dive into, than to say: I apprehend that by extreme age, the wood (and those other adjuncts) glue, parchment, paper, linings of cloth (as some use) but above all the varnish; these are all so very much (by time) dried, lenefied, made gentle, rarified, or (to say better, even) airified; so that that stiffness, stubbornness, or clunguiness, which is natural to such bodies, are so debilitated, and made playable, that the pores of the wood have a more and free liberty to move, stir, or secretly vibrate; by which means the air (which is the life of all things both animate and inanimate) has a more free and easy recourse, and to pass, and re-pass etc.—whether I have hit upon the right cause, I know not; but sure I am, *that age adds goodness to instruments*; therefore they have the advantage of all our late workmen.

An estimate of the length of time necessary 'to season the tone of the most famous makers' instruments' is given in *The Violin-makers of the Guarneri family*.[1] A violin by Stainer (the foremost non-Italian maker of the seventeenth century: he lived near Innsbruck) may have been ready from ten to fifteen years after it was made, an average sized Amati in from twenty to twenty-five years, while a more robust type would probably have needed up to thirty-five years. A long model Stradivari would require forty to fifty years, the most representative of Guarneri del Gesu's violins fifty to sixty years, and the most massive instruments of Carlo Bergonzi up to about eighty years. This conjecture, say the Hills, was based on taking into account

> that as a general rule the 'old violin' was not subjected during its maturing stage to continuous and vigorous use for a definite series of years. The tone-seasoning process has in most cases been carried out in intermittent fashion owing to the limitations inherent to the pursuit of violin-playing and the vicissitudes common to human life, which would cause an instrument to be laid aside at times, changed for another, used but little or only feebly, and seldom allowing ten years to be devoted without a break to playing it up. Use, which implies age as well, is the real factor in maturing the tone: for age without use, though it does season the fabric, cannot to the same extent improve its sound, or promote the necessary fusion between player and instrument. The negative result obtained by making violins of exceptionally old wood, an experiment tried by several French makers, is, so we believe, sufficient confirmation that our opinion is correct.

In support of their view that it is not simply age, but playing-in which seasons the tone of the instrument, the authors cite the early nineteenth-century virtuoso Ludwig Spohr as saying, of the great violins he had seen at Milan while on tour in Italy in 1816–17, that four Stradivari violins which he saw there looking new and unused, dated in fact from the master's last year, 1737, and a period some twenty years earlier than this. His comment was, however (and note that he was referring to violins then from eighty to a hundred years old):

---

[1] W. H. Hill, A. F. Hill and A. E. Hill, *The Violin-makers of the Guarneri family*. William E. Hill & Sons (London, 1965, 1st ed. 1931), 108–11.

Their tone is full and powerful, but still new and woody, and they must be played on for ten years at least to become first-rate.

And as the authors put it, the fact that such a powerful player as Spohr thought he would need ten years to play them in would be taken as equivalent to forty or more years of the intermittent playing they had described.

Reminder about the television programmes

Programme 2 is devoted to looking at the bowed and plucked string instruments and Programme 3 to looking at the woodwind instruments, commonly used in the seventeenth and eighteenth centuries. We examine the instruments at close quarters, and listen to them play. You will benefit most from these programmes if you have read the broadcast notes beforehand.

Michel de la Barre and the Hotteterre brothers, painting ascribed to Robert Tourniere's (National Gallery)

4.4 The Wind Instruments

Although the instruments of the orchestra may be divided into the strings, woodwind, brass and percussion, when considering each of these groups in more detail, 'wind' and 'brass' are seen to be inadequate terms of classification. By comparison with the wind and brass instruments, the strings are relatively straightforward in their development: the violin, viola, 'cello and double bass belong to the same family, they developed at more or less the same time (the late sixteenth century) and the principle of playing them is the same, though obviously the application of the principle to the size of the instruments resulted in individual modifications. The woodwind and brass, however, are not all closely related. The attraction of writing for these instruments stems to a great extent from the tonal contrast one obtains between them, and also, rather more noticeably than in the case of stringed instruments, the contrast between particular registers of the same instrument. The distinctive tone-qualities of the instruments with which we are familiar in the wind and brass sections of the orchestra are the result of many factors, amongst which must be considered:

(i) the means by which the sound is produced initially (i.e. the kind of mouthpiece);

(ii) whether the bore of the instrument is cylindrical or conical;

(iii) the width of the bore relative to its total length;

(iv) whether the finger holes are large or small, or whether the pitch is changed by means of valves or a sliding extension of the tube;

(v) the material out of which the instrument is made.

We have observed how in violin-making the principle and basic form of the instrument were to continue in use with comparatively little alteration after it had been established by the Brescian masters, and by the Amatis in Cremona. It was a matter of refining that form. The history of wind instruments since the seventeenth century is one of constant modification and development, the combination of the craftsman's ingenuity and a sense of artistic style. Admittedly, I think there is little which approaches the immensely satisfying form of a violin. But one responds with great admiration to the elegant line of an eighteenth-century oboe, for instance, and the immaculate and confident winding of a horn, just as one warms to the maker who has succeeded in creating an instrument which not only sounds well but is satisfying to hold and play, and is also attractive to look at.

The average eighteenth-century musician was far less conservative than the average musician today, and the concert and opera audiences of that period were generally much keener on hearing new works than we are now. The historian Burney's not infrequent observation, that a particular piece had the additional attraction of novelty to recommend it, often implied that once the novelty had worn off it would lose its popularity (which in most cases was in fact what happened). This typifies the attitude of the listener then, who expected every piece of music to be something of a new experience. In practice, even if he was hearing a sonata or a concerto for the hundredth time he was, in fact, having an experience which was not entirely predictable, since the realization of the figured bass part and the ornamentation might differ even quite significantly from performance to performance. In keeping with this desire for novelty, the rise in popularity of wind instruments, particularly of the new oboe and bassoon during the closing decades of the seventeenth century, is a factor of importance in the development of orchestral writing, in that these new instruments were ready in time for the initial experiments according to what might be termed the concerto principle.

2 keyed oboe in boxwood, c. 1740, by Bizey, Paris (Morley Pegge Collection, University of Oxford Music Faculty)

Exercise

Listen to the slow movement of Albinoni *Concerto op. 9 no. 2* on Baroque Music III side 2 band 2.

1 Albinoni makes a feature of something which the oboe is particularly good at. What is it?

2 Suggest why this is more suited to the oboe than the violin.

Oboe, from plate in Johan Christopher Weigel's Musicialisches Theatrum (Courtesy Barenreiter)

My Comments

1 In this expressive slow movement the oboe has many long holding notes, which the player can vary in tone and volume. The oboe has a great capacity

for increasing the tone from very quiet to loud, graduating the ascent throughout a long note.

2 This is possible on a violin too, of course, but an oboist can hold and build up a note longer than a violinist can with a single bow. This slow movement could be played to good effect with a violin taking the solo part instead of an oboe, but the tonal contrast achieved between the soloist and the accompanying strings and harpsichord would not be as great, and this is an attractive element of the music.

4.4.1 The Early Oboe and Bassoon

In the 1650s Jean Hotteterre, a wood turner, and Michael Philidor, who, although he was not an instrument maker was probably the instigator of the idea, began to modify the one-piece body of the treble shawm.[1] Roughly conical, this was divided into three pieces joined in the tenon-and-socket manner which was commonly used in bagpipe-making. The tapering of the conical bore could thus be achieved with far greater accuracy, and incidentally two other advantages were gained: (i) a new clarity of tone was obtained as the inside surface could be polished smooth; and (ii) by means of the tenon-and-socket joints one instrument could be tuned to another—the musician drawing the pieces apart slightly to flatten the pitch. The reed was taken firmly between the lips, instead of vibrating freely in the player's mouth as with the shawm.

Now for the first time it was directly controllable by varying the lip pressure on it, and as a result of removing the tip of the reed from the back of the mouth to just behind the teeth *tonguing* was made an effective means of articulation.[2] The forerunner of the oboe, the shawm, was already known in England by the name 'hautbois' and 'hoboy'.[3] The new instrument, therefore, while still called 'hautbois' in the country of its invention, was referred to as the 'ffranch hoboy' in England for the sake of differentiation.

It made its début at the court of Louis XIV of France towards the end of the 1650s, and some fifteen years later was introduced into England, the occasion most probably being the production in 1674 by the French composer Robert Cambert of the masque *Caloisto*, when four of Cambert's countrymen were brought to play 'hoboyes' in the orchestra.[4] The new instrument is mentioned in a comedy by Sir George Etheredge only two years later. Medley, a gentleman about town, asks two society ladies, in *The Man of Mode, or Sir Fopling Flutter* (1676):

> Are you of the number of ladies whose ears are grown so delicate since our operas that you can be charmed with nothing but flutes douces and French hautboys?[5]

[1] See *MI*, 233–4.

[2] Eric Halfpenny, 'The English 2-and 3-keyed Hautboy' *Galpin Society Journal*, I, p. 10. For *tonguing*, see *NDM*.

[3] A. Baines, *Woodwind Instruments & their History* (Faber & Faber Ltd. London, 1957), p. 237.

[4] Eric Halfpenny, 'The English Début of the French Hoboy', *Monthly Musical Record*, June 1949.

[5] Act 2. Sc. 1. (the 'flutes douces' being recorders).

The first-known oboe tutor-book in English, the *Sprightly Companion*, appeared in 1695 'Printed by J. Heptinstall, for Henry Playford: London'. At this date the few musicians who had hoboys in England must have been playing on imported French instruments. The earliest surviving hoboys made in England were built by Thomas Stanesby, whose instruments date from the first decade of the eighteenth century. Another craftsman, however, who may have made hoboys at an earlier date but of whose work nothing has survived, introduced himself with this deliberately comprehensive trade card:

John Ashbury, Sworn Servant in Ordinary to his Most Sacred Maj[tie] King William & Major Hautboy to his Own Regim[t] of Foot Guards, Makes all sorts of Wind Musical Instruments, viz[t] Flutes, Hautboys, Bassoons, &c. . . . allso turns all manner of Curious works in any sort of hard Wood or Ivory and setts in Artificiall Teeth at his House at ye Corner of Peters Court in St. Martins Lane in the Fields.[1]

We do not know the exact date of this card, though it must have been printed before the death of King William in 1702. The important thing to observe is that some twenty-five years after the hoboy was heard for the first time in England two London craftsmen were able to earn their living partly through making and selling a sufficient number of hoboys, bassoons and recorders.

More and more wind-instrument makers gradually established themselves in London, and although most of them made wind instruments of all kinds, the competition between them encouraged specialization in the building of one or two particular instruments. The name of Peter Bressan is thus associated with the recorder and the flute, the Potter family with the flute, Wood and Stanesby with the bassoon, and so on. The number of instruments of this period which have survived and are now kept in collections throughout Europe and North America indicate that there must have been quite a demand for them at the time—not only by professional players at court and at the opera, but also for use in military music, and in church bands as well as for the entertainment of amateurs. In aristocratic circles there was a fashionable interest in all things musical, so much so that in about 1710, for example, Kytsch, later to become Handel's leading oboist, could be invited to play at two and even three private parties an evening in London.[2]

The oboe and bassoon were more the professional player's instruments than the amateur's, probably because of the difficulty of making reeds. The amateur who needed a new reed only occasionally did not get the practice necessary to gain experience in the art of reed making. It is an art which requires patience as well as skill, and is undoubtedly encouraged or not by what players usually do in the country in which one lives. It is possible to buy the materials for making reeds much more easily now than it would have been for, say, an amateur in the eighteenth century living in a provincial region. Even so, although many oboists in Great Britain make reeds for their own use (and for their pupils often, too), most bassoon players here prefer to buy them—but in the United States bassoonists traditionally like to rely on having a supply of reeds which they have made themselves.

[1] L. G. Langwill, 'London Wind-Instrument Makers of the Seventeenth and Eighteenth Centuries', *The Musical Review*, May 1946, p. 88.

[2] A. Baines, *ibid.*, p. 280, quoting Burney in Rees's *Cyclopaedia*, London, 1819.

You have an opportunity of seeing and hearing what the Baroque oboe was like in the third television programme. What will strike you, probably, about its appearance is how little keywork it has (see *MI* plate 22 for the three-key oboe), and this was how the instrument was to remain until the late eighteenth century.

Exercise

This exercise is intended to draw attention to two of the most striking qualities which the oboe has. Listen in particular to the articulation used, and note the kind of music which is being played. How would you differentiate between them?

Telemann *Sonata no. 4* Vivace
Play Baroque Music II side 2 band 8

Albinoni *Concerto op. 9 no. 2* Adagio
Play Baroque Music III side 2 band 2

My Comment

These movements draw your attention to the two most characteristic qualities of the oboe: the Telemann to its sharp staccato (short, detached notes), and the Albinoni, again, to its suitability for the long legato melody.

The bassoon's history may be drawn parallel with that of the oboe, although precisely what the bassoon for which Bertoli wrote his sonatas (1645) was like is not clear. The eighteenth-century bassoon and its immediate ancestor, the dulcian, are shown in the third television programme. Like the oboe of the period, the bassoon had a minimal amount of keywork, a fact one cannot avoid being struck by when the instrument is compared with its modern counterpart. Today the bassoon is a masterpiece of mechanization, with the player's left thumb operating ten keys, to point to an extreme example.

Players of the bassoon have traditionally had problems in keeping every note in tune. Its imperfect intonation is an inherent weakness of the instrument. But bassoonists have traditionally also been good at 'lipping' bad notes into tune. This means that by slight changes in the grip of the reed in between his lips the player alters the pitch of a note up or down. The modern mechanization, particularly of the German-system bassoon (as opposed to the French system, about which you'll be reading shortly in *MI*), to a great extent corrects the instrument's intonation problems and makes it easier for the player to tackle music in keys with many sharps and flats. Bassoonists in the eighteenth century, however, were by no means confined to playing 'easy' music in the simpler keys. There are solo pieces of the period which are difficult for today's virtuoso players, notwithstanding the advantages gained through the mechanisation of the instrument.

Exercise

Listen to a movement of J. E. Galliard's *Sonata no. 3*, on Baroque Music II side 2 band 2. It is not a virtuoso piece, but it is well written for the instrument and shows what the eighteenth-century bassoon was good at rather nicely.

This movement makes a feature of three of the bassoon's most admirable characteristics. What are they?

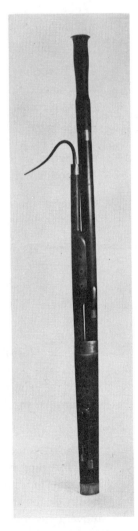

6 keyed bassoon in maple, c. 1770, by Grenser, Dresden (Bate Collection, University of Oxford Music Faculty)

Answer

1 The bassoon's agility. The movement is fast, and the main thematic material includes some sprightly hopping of an octave and of a seventh.

2 The instrument is effective playing staccato. Many composers have exploited this, with the result that the bassoon has gained a reputation for being a 'humorous' instrument.

3 Its singing, expressive tone in legato melodies (bars 10–11, 31–2, 38–9).

Check these points in the score, in unit 10.

Further Comment

Only relatively seldom did oboes and bassoons have parts written specifically for them during the early eighteenth century. Pictures and literary references make it clear, nevertheless, that they were frequently involved in both chamber and orchestral music—and in surprisingly large numbers too. They doubled the strings on the ripieno parts; there would be perhaps as many as four or five oboes and two or three bassoons in a moderately sized orchestra. This may strike us as surprising on two accounts: (i) we are used to hearing only a pair of oboes, with each on a separate part, in much orchestral music; (ii) the oboe with which we are familiar has a penetrating, individually recognizable tone, which suits it to the solo playing it has in orchestral and chamber music.

The Baroque oboe is not as loud as the modern instrument—or, perhaps, it is more accurate to say it does not have the same penetrating power. Its tone is full and round, which makes it a good mixer, both with other oboes and with different instruments. The oboe and the bassoon could add body to the ripieno strings and continuo without obtruding. They had, nevertheless, distinctive properties which made them attractive solo instruments—as you have seen in Albinoni's writing for the oboe, and Galliard's for the bassoon.

Of the composers who wrote specifically for oboes and bassoons, Handel's great output includes some of the most memorable music.

The impression which still lingers on from the bigger-and-better days of nineteenth-century Handel performances is of Handel the creator of magnificent, large-scale, imposing music, as an example of which the 'Hallelujah Chorus' springs to mind. This is to see one side only of his genius. Here, providing a view of his energy and attractive turn of phrase, in music of a less uplifting kind (perhaps you find the 'Hallelujah Chorus' even intimidating), is the little Hornpipe from the *Water Music*. It is scored for oboes, bassoons, strings and continuo. We shall look at this not only with a view to noting the use of the woodwind, but also in order to consider further the matter of form in Baroque music.

Baroque dance movements are generally in two-part, or binary, form. You can see this if you look at the scores of the dance movements we have on record: the Hornpipe from Handel's *Water Music*, the Allemande of Bach's third suite for unaccompanied cello, and the Rigaudon by the French composer Joseph Bodin de Boismortier, in his *Petites Sonates op. 66 no. 4*. Each of these dance movements falls into two sections separated by a double bar with repeat signs (the two dots). In the case of dance music actually meant for dancing the repeats would be observed, otherwise it was up to the performers how they repeated. Such a short movement as the fast, sixteen-bar Hornpipe from the *Water Music* obviously needs some repetition or it would be over and done with far too quickly. In our recording it is taken three times through without stopping at the double bar in the middle, each repetition distinguished by a change in orchestration, strings only first, then oboes and bassoons and finally all together.

Listen to this movement, following the score in unit 10 as you do so.

Handel *Water Music* Hornpipe

Play Baroque Music III side 1 band 3

The music moves quickly, and the bright, strongly rhythmic effect is heightened by the incisive playing of the oboes and bassoons. Let us look at what happens, bar by bar, considering the rhythmic configuration of the melody right through.

The melody can be broken up into these fragments:

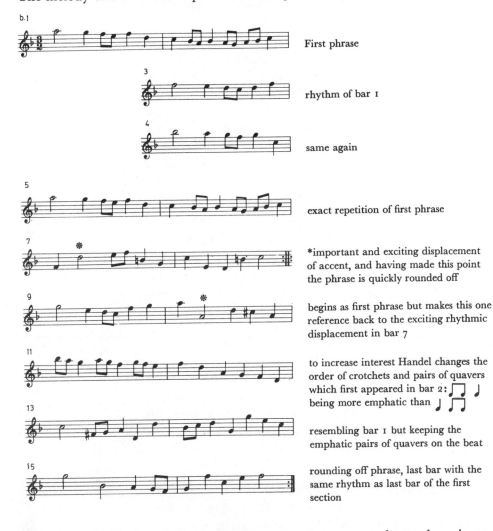

b.1 — First phrase

3 — rhythm of bar 1

4 — same again

5 — exact repetition of first phrase

7 — *important and exciting displacement of accent, and having made this point the phrase is quickly rounded off

9 — begins as first phrase but makes this one reference back to the exciting rhythmic displacement in bar 7

11 — to increase interest Handel changes the order of crotchets and pairs of quavers which first appeared in bar 2: being more emphatic than

13 — resembling bar 1 but keeping the emphatic pairs of quavers on the beat

15 — rounding off phrase, last bar with the same rhythm as last bar of the first section

The main rhythmic stresses do not come on every strong beat: there is no feeling of emphasis on the first beat of every bar. If there were, there would be little feeling of 'flow' in the music. In fact it races along so lightly you are hardly aware of when one phrase ends and the next one begins. When you have listened to the movement a few times and followed the score with it, try humming the melody at a slower pace. You will find it falls into phrases of regular length, except for where the normal length of phrase breaks into two. If the vertical lines represent bar lines, here is the pattern of phrases:

In this very short movement we can see Handel's happy knack of generating melody as he goes along out of what has just gone before. The secret of success lies in the uncomplicated rhythmic repetition. The beginning of section A and the beginning of section B in a binary-form movement conventionally have some melodic resemblance. In the Hornpipe you can see how the first four notes of each section make a similar downward swoop, then turn up.

After that similarity ends, but because the *rhythmic* shape is the same in both these fragments it gives us the assurance that we have heard it before, even though we have not exactly in that form. In a movement as short as this in which we have hardly had time to forget this particular rhythmic pattern which we heard last only four bars earlier, such a melodic connection between the openings of each section is not necessary. In longer binary-form movements, however, it served to give the listener his bearings. If the melody was not heard on the top, it might be placed in the bass, or possibly the melodic contour of the melody might be *inverted*, with for example a phrase which rises and gradually falls being changed into one that falls then rises gradually. You will be meeting examples of melodic inversion later.

The first section of a binary-form movement conventionally ends in a different key from the one in which it begins. Major-key movements usually modulate into the dominant key, thus a movement beginning in C major would by the end of the first section have modulated into its dominant G major, while movements in a minor key tend to modulate to the relative major, that is for example, A minor would modulate to C major, the major key with which it shares the same key signature. By the end of the second section the music has to be brought back into the 'home' key again. The Hornpipe is in F major. To get to C major, its dominant key, the B flat in the scale of F major has to be eliminated and B natural, the important leading-note in the scale of C major, introduced—which happens in bar 7. You will notice that in the second half there are C sharps and later F sharps, when Handel modulates into other keys to provide interest on his way home, passing through D minor and G minor respectively.

The two sections of this Hornpipe are of equal length, but it is more usual for the second section of a binary-form movement to be longer than the first. Before we go on to look at a movement in which this is the case, would you listen to the Hornpipe as many times as may be necessary for you to note all the points I have just mentioned.

Play Baroque Music III side 1 band 3

Exercise

Listen to Baroque Music II side 2 band 9, and without referring to the score, describe the form of the dance played.

Discussion

What we have here is a pair of binary-form movements so arranged that, overall, a *ternary* arrangement is obtained. Thus, the first Rigaudon, in the minor key, is in two sections A and B, both of which are repeated, and, you ought to have noticed, with the B section much longer than A. Then comes a major-key Rigaudon of the same length and form, after which we hear the first Rigaudon again without repeats. It is exactly the same overall shape as the Minuet and Trio with which you are familiar from all the Classical symphonies you know.

This charming and innocuous little piece was chosen as an example of one of the lesser-known forms of Baroque music. Unlike the great and memorable concerto movements, this pair of dances, and literally thousands like it, sank almost without trace towards the end of the eighteenth century. Joseph Bodin de Boismortier, its composer, wrote about a hundred such duet sonatas which were published in beautifully engraved editions for the use of gentlemen players. Duet music of this kind, conventionally with a wide choice of instrumentation offered, was one of the very few types of composition which did not use or require the support of continuo instruments.

If you refer now to the score you will see that the first Riguadon is in D minor. The B flat needed for the key is not put in the key-signature but notated each time as an accidental. From the home key of D minor we are not, as we might expect, given the security of a clear perfect cadence into the new key. Instead, Boismortier brings us to a pause on the *dominant note*, A, while still remaining in the home key of D minor. Immediately after the double bar the music is in the relative major key of F major, in which it continues and reaffirms with a perfect cadence in F at bar 16. The C sharp necesssary as the leading-note in the home key of D minor is introduced in the following bar. The second Rigaudon, in the tonic major key, D major, sounds fresher and is rather livelier. Here again there is no modulation at the end of the first section, only a brief stopping on the dominant chord while still in D major. The conventional modulation to the dominant key, A major in this case, does eventually come in the middle of the section. There is a perfect cadence in A major at bar 16, but we are immediately taken back into the home key afterwards. In the opening figures of both dances the characteristic rhythmic accentuation of the Rigaudon ♩ | ♩ ♩ | ♩ is felt. In neither dance, however, does this composer make any resemblance between the openings of the first and second sections.

When you are sure you have followed the movement and have understood the points made, turn to the Allemande from Bach's third suite for unaccompanied cello. We have already seen how this ornate but energetic movement is idiomatically written for the cello, and commented on some of the features of interest. We shall look now at its form: you can make your own analysis. The music is printed in unit 10 and a performance is recorded on Baroque Music II side 2 band 6.

Exercise

1 Comment on the proportionate length of sections A and B in this binary-form movement.

2 Is there any melodic resemblance between the openings of A and B?

3 Where do you feel the main rhythmic stresses fall? Say whether you are counting in four or eight.

4 If you are able to comment on the key scheme, do so.

My Comments

1 They are of equal length, twelve bars each.

2 Yes, there is: the beginning of section B is exactly the same as the opening except that it is now in another key. You should *hear* this, and by referring to the score it is not difficult to spot. We have noted earlier what a fine opening gesture this is. Covering two octaves, it moves with a compelling rhythm which pushes forward to the next group following, so that the first note in each rhythmic group is emphasized. What are these notes? Notes from the tonic chord of C major in the first bar.

3 I have already answered this above. I count four, not a quick eight in the bar, in this movement. The main stresses, though barely perceptible from the weight on each beat, come on One-two-Three-four.

4 Beginning in C major, and establishing this clearly by emphasizing in the first bar the component parts of the tonic chord, there is a cadence again in C major in the middle of bar 4 after which we quickly slip into G major—you see the F sharp introduced in bar 5—and the closing cadence of section A is in G major, the dominant key. The opening figure is then transposed exactly into G major, extending as far as the bottom G only, after which Bach gives the cello an interval not of an octave (as in bar 1, beat 5) but of a tenth (bar 13, beat 4). From G major the music passes to A minor after a long preparation of three bars on the dominant chord of E major for the cadence which comes in bar 17. It then quickly passes through F major and its own relative minor, D minor (bar 19), through C major, to F major and back 'home' to C major again.

You may be finding this difficult. But do try to work it out, and not take it on trust. It is important to realize that in music from the period we are looking at onward, up to the present (apart from *atonal* music) the relationship of keys with one another within a movement, is fundamental to the structure. In this Allemande for cello solo Bach modulates to the dominant, passes through some of the other keys which are most closely related to it, and returns to the home key. The Hornpipe by Handel has the same scheme: beginning in F major, it modulates to the dominant, C major, at the double bar, then passes through D minor and G minor, two closely related keys.

The modulations we have observed here are, in fact, typical not only of the short dance movements of this period but of longer movements too, as we shall see when we analyse some sonata and concerto movements.

4.4.2 Flute and Recorder

The flute and recorder had existed side by side in music-making in the sixteenth and seventeenth centuries. But towards the end of this period the flute was changed fundamentally by craftsmen of the Hotteterre family, the bore which had previously been cylindrical being cut slightly conical, tapering away from the 'blowing end'. The new flute had a most attractive, rich tone, and from the beginning of the eighteenth century it grew steadily in popularity, especially with 'gentlemen' players, notwithstanding the traditional antipathy for the instrument. It is difficult to understand why there has always been a strong anti-flute faction,[1] but several composers have shared this attitude, not least Mozart, and Berlioz especially, whose most insulting epithet was 'flute-player'.

---

[1] My colleague, Gerald Hendrie, offers the interesting suggestion that possibly it stems from the fact that it was not felt proper for men to play it in Greek times perhaps because its pure tone was reminiscent of a boy's voice.

The early eighteenth-century flute is not a loud instrument, and it has only limited carrying power. The modern instrument by comparison has a much brighter tone, and can play loudly without going out of tune. The Baroque flute's intonation suffers if it is forced to play more loudly than its makers had ever intended it to be played, and because circumstances demanded that the flute should take a place in the Classical symphony orchestra, where it had to be played hard to be heard—and in consequence almost inevitably sounded out of tune—it came to have rather a bad name. Burney, his opinion coloured thus by a late eighteenth-century acquaintance with the instrument, wrote unenthusiastically about one of the first flute virtuosos to appear in England:

> Wiedemann, who came to England, about the year 1726, was long the principal solo player on the German-flute. He was a good musician; but in his productions, he never broke through the bounds of that mediocrity to which his instrument seems confined.[1]

Recorder player, by F. Kupetsky (Budapest Museum of Fine Arts)

[1] *BH*, ii, 1015.

The flute, for the hard-blowing players of the Classical era, was, in fact, to remain an unsatisfactory instrument, and did so well on into the nineteenth century until Boehm of Munich built his revolutionary model (1847) which achieved both a loud, full tone and good intonation.

The Baroque flute is no louder than a recorder—which in the eighteenth century was known as the common flute. Both instruments are capable of playing in a very agile manner, but the flute can play slow, sustained music in a more expressive way than the recorder. From the turn of the century composers were showing the transverse flute to be an ideal instrument for *Affettuoso* movements (slow movements of a highly expressive nature), and this aspect tipped the scales in its favour in competition with the recorder. As a result, it was the flute, not the recorder, which went on to establish itself as a permanent member of the Classical orchestra. The various sizes of recorder, nevertheless, continued to be played, if mostly by amateurs, up to the end of the century, and instruction books for the 'common flute' were issued to provide for them.

Baroque music can usually be played on either flute or treble recorder. It is seldom that the one instrument has even to adapt the part to get all the notes in. This consequently leads to problems of deciding (now) which instrument

Handel, for instance, had in mind when he wrote an obligato part for 'flauti' in an opera, or for which instrument Bach wrote the two solo parts in his *Fourth Brandenburg Concerto*. In general one goes by the title; in English music a recorder was intended unless 'flute' was qualified by calling it a 'German flute' or a 'transverse flute' (because it was held sideways). On the continent too, 'flauti' generally meant recorders, at least up to the mid-eighteenth century, while 'traverso' was the flute. The '*flûtes douces*' of the *Fourth Brandenburg Concerto* are most commonly played by flutes now, but small-sized recorders were probably intended, sounding an octave higher than written and having a gentle ('douce') tone.

I have spoken of the Baroque period in music as the age of the violin, and have given greater prominence to the violin and to the other members of the violin family, because these are the instruments for which by far the greater part of significant Baroque music was written. But having said that, and also having now referred to the flute, oboe and bassoon of the period, it must be seen that these were important too; oboes and bassoons were commonly used on the ripieno parts of concertos, and both these instruments and the flute were scored for in a considerable body of chamber music. The Germans, in particular, wrote many trio sonatas in which the oboe and flute took the melodic parts, as alternatives to the more common pair of violins. The trio sonata movement by Quantz, which you have on record, is a typical example. Johann Joachim Quantz (1697–1773) was court musician and flute teacher to King Frederick the Great of Prussia.

Waldhorn (Weigel, Musi-calisches Theatrum, courtesy Barenreiter)

Exercise

1 By listening without reference to the score, decide what the melodic characteristics are of the Allegro from the C minor trio sonata by Quantz. Is the main tune on the flute which we hear at the beginning smooth, vigorous, energetic, languid, nervous—or what? Does it move fairly consistently by short steps or does it hop around?

2 Make a note of the recurring pattern of strong and weak stresses which run right through the movement with little let-up.

3 Are the phrases of the flute melody at the beginning long or short? By relating to the pattern of stresses you found for question 2, indicate the length of the phrases that the flute tune falls into.

Play Baroque Music II side 1 band 3

Answers

1 Of the descriptive words in question 1, I should *not* have applied 'smooth' or 'languid' to this melody. For the most part, movement is a mixture of scalic runs and wider intervals; the general impression I get is that the short-step movement tends to predominate and that in fact it is a pretty static tune really. You will see my reasons for saying this in the following exercise.

2 If you should count quickly with the record, sub-dividing each beat, the stress pattern which runs through the whole movement with only occasional relief is ONE-and-two-AND-ONE-and-two-AND- etc. or, if you prefer to see it in music notation,

3 Short. The rests in the melody help to give the answer.

This fragmentation of the melody in the opening bars makes for a nervous, slightly hesitant line, but the overall character of the movement quite contradicts this.

Exercise

1 Quantz wrote in his flute treatise that

> the most beautiful melody will in the end prove a soporific if it is never relieved, and continuous liveliness and unmitigated difficulty arouse astonishment but do not move particularly.[1]

Describe how Quantz provides relief and keeps your attention.

2 Refer to the score of this movement which is in unit 10, then after listening carefully to the opening tune (get to know it, be able to sing it through) think about the recurring stress pattern which we refer to in question 2 of the foregoing exercise. These stresses emphasize certain notes of the melody. Decide which these notes are—sing them, or if you can, write them in on the stave below.

[1] *SRMH*, 591.

Answers

1 Quantz makes use of the built-in contrast that is provided in the trio sonata by having not one but *two* equal melody instruments; in our case the flute and oboe are even more useful than the two violins more frequently scored for, since there is more difference between them tonally than one would get between two violins. Besides contrasting the two melodic instruments by giving them similar passages alternately, there is also the possibility of course of contrasting solo passages with passages of a fuller texture with both oboe and flute playing together.

There are *tuneful* sections, and sections which are less obviously tuneful—like bars 80–6 for example—in which Quantz works what is a *harmonic* figure in imitation between the two wind instruments. The flute and oboe do not play *a tune* in imitation, but a figure which is a decoration of the chords used. Elsewhere, bars 38–49 and 64–70, we do not hear a melodic line but passages in which that simple scalic run from bar 7 at the beginning is passed around. Perhaps you had the impression that while some passages are tuneful others are rather obviously 'filling' in between them.

2

In the second bar the A♭ is a decoration, leaning on to the G which is the essential note there. It is the same in the third bar, and the fourth. The essential note is the G all along, which, being the dominant degree of the scale of C minor which this piece is in, has the rather bright quality that all dominants tend to be endowed with.

4.4.3 The Clarinet

The clarinet had to wait longer than the oboe, bassoon and flute to become accepted as a permanent member of the orchestra, and in fact it hardly figures in Baroque music at all. I shall say a brief word about it here all the same, so that you will be familiar with its history by the time you read the following units on the symphony. We do not have any examples of music in which a clarinet is included on the Baroque music records.

The clarinet was introduced to France and England in pieces of an 'out of doors' character in the mid-eighteenth century, two clarinets often being matched by a pair of horns. Clarinets were built in various sizes (like the recorder, but, generally, unlike the oboe or the bassoon), those in A, B♭, C and F being used, with clarinets built in B♭ and C predominating during the eighteenth century. The origin of the clarinet has for a long time been the cause of dispute, although it is generally held that the instrument was invented by the Nürnberg instrument-maker J. C. Denner (1655–1707) in about 1700. Carse says this is probably true, but questions the idea that he based it on a development of the chalumeau, and that the chalumeau was a primitive clarinet. Referring to a work published in 1730 by the historian Doppelmayr, he writes:[1]

> . . . this book contains an account of Johann Christoph Denner, a flute-maker, and includes the statement that Denner invented the 'so-called' clarinet at the beginning of the 18th century; later on it is also stated that he eventually improved the chalumeau and other instruments. This reads as if Denner accomplished two things; he invented one instrument, and improved another. Doppelmayr's account of Denner was repeated word for word by Walther in his Lexikon, who also added some information about the clarinet and, incidentally, managed to contradict himself when giving the compass of the new instrument. Walther's description was repeated in almost the same words by Eisel in 1738 and by Majer in 1741. Since then, the statement that Denner invented the clarinet, has been handed on from book to book, and from one musical dictionary to another, till in the course of time there was added to it the gratuitous information that Denner's clarinet has been based on the chalumeau. Doppelmayr's statements that Denner invented the clarinet, and that he also improved the chalumeau, provide no evidence for supposing that the clarinet was an improved chalumeau, or even for assuming that the latter was an instrument of the single reed family. There is no reason to doubt the correctness of the information supplied by Doppelmayr; his book, which must have taken a long time to compile, was published at Nürnberg only twenty-three years after Denner's death; in it he states that two sons of Denner, whom he does not name, successfully carried on their father's craft in the same town after his death. But for Doppelmayr, the name of the originator of the clarinet would never have been known, for there is no independent evidence to support his statement. All the later writers took their information from Walther, who in turn had it from Doppelmayr.

In spite of the fact that Praetorius, Mersenne and other 17th century writers appear to have known nothing of the instrument on which Denner is alleged to have based his clarinet, it is not unreasonable to suppose that some such instrument with a cylindrical tube and a single reed was used in Europe before the 18th century, and that Denner did not create a new type. The logical course of events would be that the primitive type existed before the more advanced type, but the hard fact must be faced, that no trace of the chalumeau as it was described in the 18th century by Diderot and Reynvaan can be found before Denner's time.

That Denner began to improve the chalumeau in 1690, or that the clarinet dates from that or any other specific year, are amongst several estimates made by 19th-century writers which have eventually been cited as facts, and have been repeated over and over again, but in support of which no historical evidence can be produced. . . .

If Denner based his clarinet on some single-reed instrument of more primitive type, his vital discovery was, that by opening a vent-hole near the upper end of the tube, the scale of fundamentals might be made to sound a twelfth higher.

5 keyed clarinet in C, made of boxwood by Longman and Broderip, London c. 1780 (Bate Collection, University of Oxford Music Faculty)

[1] A. Carse, *Musical Wind Instruments* (Macmillan, London, 1939), 150-1.

*Mouthpiece and reed of
clarinet shown opposite*

We need to note two particular factors about the clarinet. First: its fingering system is not based on overblowing at the octave. Such overblowing means that if a note in the lowest register of the instrument is fingered and one blows differently, concentrating a tighter jet of breath over the mouth-hole of a flute for example, one sounds the note an octave higher. Now, as you read in Carse, the clarinet overblows at the twelfth above the note fingered in the lowest register, a factor which endows each register with an even more markedly distinctive tone quality than in other wind instruments, because these registers are farther apart.

Second: the matter of transposition. The clarinet was subjected to much scaling up and down in size in an attempt to gain the best tone. Rather than make it necessary for the player to remember a different set of fingerings for each of these, fingering C for instance, one way on a clarinet of this size and in another on that, a single set of fingerings was applied to all sizes of the instrument. The result was that whereas on one size of clarinet the note which sounded was C, if the player fingered his C, on other sizes of instrument the actual pitch of the sound which came out of the clarinet when he fingered C might be D, E flat, B flat or A. For the sake of identification, the clarinet which sounded B flat when the player fingered his C was known as a 'clarinet in B flat', and the clarinet which sounded A when he fingered his C a 'clarinet in A'. Now, the other woodwind instruments about which I have spoken are 'in C', i.e. if the player sees, for example, the note G on the copy and fingers his G, the note which we hear is also G (which means that the oboist may play a flute part or, of more importance in the eighteenth century, a violin part, just as it was written as long as the compass of his instrument allowed it). These are said to be *non-transposing* instruments. The clarinet on the other hand is a *transposing* instrument, which makes for a slight complication when a clarinettist wishes to play a violin or an oboe part, because with a clarinet in B flat, for example, everything he played would *sound* a tone lower than what is written, although the player is fingering the right notes as far as he is concerned. So, to get him in line with the others, enabling him to play in the same key as the other players, his clarinet part has to be transposed into the key a tone *higher*: when he plays then from this written part, the sound we hear is in the same key as the other instruments. The sizes of clarinet which are tonally the best are those of the clarinet in B flat and in A. It is useful to bear in mind that with these clarinets, *the sound we hear is lower by a tone and a minor third respectively, than the written note for the player*. If a symphony is in F major, the part for a clarinet in B flat would be written in the key of G major.

I mentioned earlier that the double bass and violone are transposing instruments, sounding an octave lower than the written part. We meet with other transposing instruments in the eighteenth-century orchestra too: horns and trumpets, which have different intervals of transposition again. I have introduced the matter as one of the 'facts of life' of the music we are studying. I do not expect you to gain in this course the practical experience of working out the transposition of the various instruments for yourself.

We decided not to make it a prerequisite that you had to be able to read a score and at the same time hear mentally what was printed. But you are expected to be able to follow the score as you listen to music on record. As you work through the many pieces we analyse, your ability to take in more details at a time should increase, including, of course, coping with the occasional transposing instrument.

It would be useful if you now read the chapter on 'The Woodwind' in *MI*, to see how the instruments as we know them today relate to those of the period which we are studying. This is of greater importance than in the case of later developments in the violin and cello, for instance, because the actual stringed instruments have undergone little change since the early nineteenth century.

The technique of playing the violin has evolved without mechanical aids other than the addition of the chin and shoulder rest. But with woodwind playing the technique of the player and the improvements continually being brought out by rival instrument-makers are so intimately connected, that ideally we should like to spend a month demonstrating in the form of a progress report: in 1750 the flute had x keys and this was possible . . . in 1820 it was being manufactured with y keys, making it possible to play *this* with greater facility, and so on.

Collecting musical instruments has become increasingly popular in recent times, and at present it is not difficult to have access to collections which include eighteenth-century woodwind instruments. In Great Britain we are particularly indebted to the scholarly work of the *Galpin Society*, whose members not only buy and restore old instruments but write with enthusiasm and erudition about them and learn to perform on them as well. Most of the authors of the chapters we are reading in *MI* are members of the society. There are some fine collections of instruments throughout Europe and America, but the most comprehensive is the one in the *Conservatoire Royal de Musique*, Brussels, to which every enthusiast hopes to make a visit some time.

Read now *MI* pp. 237–76, paying particular attention to pages 237–47, the relevant plates, and articles in the *Glossary* as necessary.

For a detailed account of the trumpet and the older brass instruments, and for an explanation of *crooks* and what they did, read *MI* 277–94. Read also and consider the section pp. 295–302, in the chapter on 'The Horn, and the Later Brass', in *MI*.

1.4.4 The Brass

While the stringed instruments appear on first sight not to have changed since the eighteenth century, a mere glance will show that the woodwind have far more keys on them now than earlier. However, the brass instruments are the most noticeably changed instruments of all. Have a look at the horns, for example, which are photographed on Plate 28 in *MI*, and decide what it is that is so different about the earlier and later models.

The important difference between the horn as it is now and as it was in the eighteenth century is that at that time *it had no valves* (such an instrument is now called a 'natural horn'). Both horns and trumpets depend for the notes within their range upon the harmonic series, about which you can read in *MI*. The essential point about these instruments is that they could not play every chromatic note of the scale. In fact, at the bottom of their compass there were gaps, and higher up two of the possible notes were out of tune. Composers therefore, for obvious practical reasons, had to know which notes were available to be used in their music since by the late eighteenth century various crooks were used.

The trumpet, like the horn, could be fitted with crooks which enabled the instrument to play in keys other than D major, the key of the harmonic series natural to the length of tubing most commonly used in the Baroque trumpet.

D major was, nevertheless, the key chosen for most music of the period which included trumpets.

Exercise

For an impression of how the trumpet was used in Baroque music, listen now to the finale of *Trumpet Concerto in D major* by Giuseppe Torelli (1658–1709).

Torelli was one of the leading composers at the end of the seventeenth century of the influential school of composers centred on the basilica of St Petronio, Bologna. These composers made a particular feature of the trumpet in sonatas and concertos like the one on record, which were played on festive occasions. This movement highlights a rather obvious feature of practically every solo sonata and solo concerto of the period. Note the register in which the trumpet plays.

Listen particularly to the soloist, and decide what it is that persuades you to concentrate your attention on him.

Play Baroque Music III side 1 band 5

My Comments

The trumpet stands out very clearly from the other instruments in that movement. Because it is tonally quite distinct—and louder too—you cannot help getting your attention fixed on it every time it comes in. A composer does not often make his soloist resort to the primitive practice of, figuratively speaking, shouting loudest to gain attention, although you can probably recall instances where this is used to dramatic effect. Instruments which are naturally louder than others do have a certain advantage in this respect, of course, if used appropriately. But more craftsmanship is shown in according the soloist greater melodic interest than the accompanying instruments, making him play,

Trumpeters and trombone players. Detail from engraving by Lepautre, The Coronation of Louis XIV at Rheims 1654 (Bibliotheque Nationale; Photo Giraudon)

perhaps, a difficult 'impressive' part or simply by giving him the most active part in the ensemble. Torelli's solo line here is not a memorable one, and at the end, the impression I retain is of the high trumpet hurrying around—though with apparent purpose—in a limited range.

Further Discussion

The part lies in the upper register of the instrument. The Bologna trumpeters were specialists at playing in the 'clarino' register, as it is called. The neglect of the St Petronio trumpet music until a few years ago may be put down to the fact that orchestral trumpet parts from the end of the eighteenth century tended not to be so high, and as a result musicians lost the art of clarino playing. Baroque composers, when using trumpets, wanted them to take part in contrapuntal textures on the same basis as other instruments. The only way they could do this was by using the high register where available notes were close enough together to make melodic lines possible. In Classical music, on the other hand, trumpets were not given contrapuntal lines. They contributed weight and volume in orchestral tuttis, often playing held notes or punctuating the rhythm with the same repeated note. Trumpet players could still make the occasional high note when required, with great effort, but Baroque trumpet parts until only recently have been regarded with concern by musicians who have not made a study of the special techniques required.

4.5 Instruments in the Early-Eighteenth century Orchestra

The general attitude of Baroque composers towards the use of instruments was an extremely practical one. The composer, who was himself often the performer or the director of the performance anyway, wrote parts for the instruments available. If these were not to hand, no great harm was done by substituting other instruments. The basic sound was strings and continuo. For variety, a pair of oboes and some bassoons could be put in to double the two top parts and the bass line. And for variety again, they could be taken off. If players turned up at a Gentlemen's Music Club with recorders or flutes, they could join in on the top parts as well. The orchestration of an opera would depend on what the composer knew he had available in his pit orchestra, and might be expected to be more specific. Even so, apart from isolated colourful effects, the orchestration of an aria, like the orchestration of a movement in a concerto, would remain more or less unchanged throughout. Between movements was thought to be the logical place to change the basic quality of the sound. The violins, divided into two parts, shared the melodic material fairly evenly and therefore if, for the sake of interest, additional instruments were to be added, they would normally reinforce *both* violin parts, not only the first violins. Thus the addition of oboes was quite usual. But, although it was not uncommon to have more than two bassoons in an orchestra, they all played from the same part (on account of the nature of the continuo).

Burney said[1] that to him, John Christian Bach appeared to be the first composer to follow as a principle the law of contrast (as he called it). Passages of contrasting nature had occurred frequently in the works of composers before Bach, but these, Burney asserted, were accidental rather than the outcome of a consistently applied principle. Thus, in a brief statement, he disposed of the whole of Baroque and Renaissance music, notwithstanding the fact that in the

[1] *BH*, ii, 866.

music of both styles *contrast*, brought about by the opposition of forces, and the interplay of different sound groups, was a salient characteristic. Nor did he add support to his pronouncement by continuing:

> Bach in his symphonies and other instrumental pieces, as well as his songs, seldom failed, after a rapid and noisy passage to introduce one that was slow and soothing.

This sort of section-balancing was the stock-in-trade procedure of the Baroque composer, whose music may be likened to many judiciously arranged blocks of sound, an image which has given rise to the expression 'terraced dynamics', about which we shall have more to say in the following units. It is for this very reason that the concerto grosso epitomizes music of the Baroque style, its concertino-ripieno structure embracing so many possibilities of block contrast as far as the 'mechanical' aspects of the composition (volume, weight, texture and sonorities, etc.) are concerned, in addition to any variation of mood which the composer wished to portray by suitable changes of expression.

Yet, Burney *had* observed something of real significance, and he was referring, of course, to a different kind of contrast. His statement about 'the London Bach' begs for qualification, and he only partly succeeds in emending it. He comments on J. C. Bach's 'variety of accompaniments', enhanced by his novel use of the full orchestra's resources, but fails to draw attention to the vital point that the instrumentation was an inseparable element of his style, not merely an embellishment of it. And this, after all, touches the heart of the matter in the stylistic

An orchestral concert at the Mariekirche, Munich, by Johan August Corvinus, c. 1715 (Munchener Stadtmuseums)

change which took place during the mid-eighteenth century. Few musicians could have realized at the time the full meaning of the development, although it was widely regarded as one of tremendous moment. It amounted to a general adoption of a new concept in place of the principles which musicians had observed in composition during the foregoing century and a half. Burney had hinted at an emphasis on attractive orchestration in John Christian's music, but this was only one facet, a very important one, of the style which was being taken up by composers throughout Europe. John Christian's kind of contrast was different from that of Baroque music. He does not simply have sectional contrasts (as in Baroque music, between full orchestra and solo group, for instance) but contrasts of a dramatic and expressive nature in which he mixes his instrumental resources far more fluently, to accommodate the continually changing character of the music.

You will be considering the other facets of the new style in the next part of the course, from which vantage point it will be easier, in contrast, to see what an essentially uncomplicated view Baroque composers had of the instrumental resources they had at their disposal.

The resources available varied enormously from court to court, and from one occasion (a small meeting of amateur players led by professionals, for example) to another (a large *ad hoc* band at a festival). The most extensive research into the constitution and strength of eighteenth-century orchestras was done by Adam Carse, and published in his *The Orchestra in the XVIIIth Century*, 1940. From the tables he derives from many different sources, we quote the figures reflecting the size of orchestras in the early part of the century.

Orchestra	Date	Violin 1st	Violin 2nd	Viola	Cello	Bass	Flute	Oboe	Clarinet	Bassoon	Horn	Trumpet	Drums	Remarks
Arnstadt (Count Anton Günther)	1690	?		?	?	?		2		1		5		Twenty-one musicians altogether
Bayreuth (Court Orchestra)	1740	27 musicians												
Bayreuth (Court Orchestra)	1742	6		1	1	?	?				3			From a painting on a table
Berlin (King of Prussia)	1712	6	5	2	5			4		3		?		
Brunswick (Hof-musik)	1731	8		1	2	1	5			3	2			'7 Trompeter so bei der Musik'
Dresden (King of Poland)	1697	6		?	?	?		6		3	3	1		Theorbo and six other instruments which are not specified
Dresden (King of Poland)	1709	4		2	4	1	2	4		2		?	?	Also 1 *Haute-contre* and 1 *Taille*, probably viols. Two theorbos
Dresden (King of Poland)	1719	7		5	5	5	2	5		3	2	?	?	One pantaleon, 2 theorbos

Orchestra	Date	Violin 1st	2nd	Viola	Cello	Bass	Flute	Oboe	Clarinet	Bassoon	Horn	Trumpet	Drums	Remarks
Dresden (King of Poland)	1731	6 ⏜		3	4	2	3	4		3	2	?	?	Two harpsichords
Dresden (King of Poland)	1734	12 ⏜		4	5	2	3	3		?	2	?	?	
Hamburg (Opera)	1738	8 ⏜		3	2	2	5	4		5	4	4	1	Viola d'amore, Gamba, 2 piccolo, 2 zuffolo, traversa bassa, quart flöte, 2 cornetti, 2 oboe d'amore, Hautbois haute-contre, 2 chalumeau, 2 trombe di caccia
Leipzig (Concert-Gesellschaft)	1746	5	5	1 (+ 2)	2	2	3 ⏜			3	2	(2	1)	One violinist also plays trumpet; 2 vocalists also play viola; 1 flautist also plays trumpet. Two horn players also play string instruments
Leipzig (Bach)	1730	3	3	2	2	1	2	2		1		2	?	Partly amateurs. The bassoon was an apprentice
London (The King's Band)	1710 to 1755	From 24 to 26 musicians												
London (Foundling Hospital) (Handel)	1759	12 ⏜		3	3	2		4		4	2	2	1	
Mannheim (Court Orchestra)	1720	12 ⏜		2	2	3	15 ⏜					?	?	Trumpets and drums available
Paris (Chapelle-Musique)	1708	6 ⏜		3*	3	(1)	2	2		1				*Music scored for three different sizes of viola. Theorbo 'Gros basson'. Theorbo player doubles on double-bass
Paris (Opéra)	1713	12 ⏜		*	8		8 hautbois, flûtes ou bassons ⏜						1	*2 1st viola; 2 2nd viola; 3 3rd viola
Vienna (Court Orchestra)	1721	23 ⏜		?	4	3		5		4	1	16	2	Gamba, lute, 2 cornetti, 4 trombones
Vienna (Court Orchestra)	1730	32 ⏜						5		5	1	13	1	Gamba, lute, theorbo, 4 trombones
Weimar (Ducal Orchestra)	1700	2 ⏜		?	1 ⏜		?	?		1		5	1	
Weimar (Ducal Orchestra)	1714	4 ⏜		?	1 ⏜		?	?		2		7	1	The 4 violins include J. S. Bach as Konzertmeister

In addition to the personnel listed, there would also have been an assortment of continuo players on harpsichord or organ, and plucked instruments. The proportion of strings committed to each part Carse averages out as approximately as follows:

Small orchestras: 2 or 3 Vn. 1^0—2 or 3 Vn 2^0—Va—1 cello—1 double bass
Medium orchestras: 4—4—2—2—2
Large orchestras: 6—6—3—3—2 or 3
Exceptional orchestras: 9 or 10—9 or 10—5—4—4

For the appropriate balance of wind parts he suggests that on the whole, the eighteenth-century orchestras employed roughly one woodwind player to three strings. He cites the figures recommended by Quantz, who advocates a slightly higher proportion of wind players:

2 Vn 1^0—2 Vn 2^0—1 Va—1 cello—1 double bass—No wind
3—3—1—1—1—One bassoon
4—4—2—2—2—2 flutes, 2 oboes, 2 bassoons ⎫
5—5—2—3—2—Ditto   ⎬horns
6—6—3—4—2—4 flutes, 4 oboes, 3 bassoons ⎭

The revival of Baroque music in recent years has gradually brought it home to musicians that the eighteenth-century orchestra was not the same as the large symphony orchestra of today, and that in the performance of this kind of music clarity of sound counts.

This is not over-stating the case: you may recall from Foundation Level the radio talk about how grossly over-orchestrated and 'modernized' the *Messiah* was during the nineteenth century.[1] We may still hear performances of the *Third Brandenburg Concerto*, for instance, played by the massed strings of this orchestra or the other. But we have also heard concertos played by small groups of players, and most of us prefer this. It is a matter of taste, of course, but if we take a scholarly view of the music based on knowledge of the performance practices of the period, it is possible to say that this performance is reasonably appropriate in so far as the numbers of players and the style of playing is concerned, while that one is not, being an inflated, possibly 'romantic' interpretation of the music.

Having scaled the ensemble to Baroque proportions, the logical step on from there is to attempt to capture the sound and the spirit of Baroque music in the performance. To do this, the musicians have to learn to play on eighteenth-century instruments and to use eighteenth-century playing techniques. The result one hopes to obtain is an 'authentic' performance. But, it stands to reason, such a performance has to be put on in the appropriate setting, preferably a music room or church in which the acoustics are rich but lively. Although the performance might be good, we would find it difficult to appreciate it if it were given by a chamber group in an enormous hall.

In attempting to 'get into' the music in an authentic way there are many difficulties to overcome. We are used to the sound of the modern instruments, which in general have a richer, heavier tone than they possessed in the eighteenth century. We may not immediately see the attractions of the smaller, sometimes coarser, sound of the earlier instrument either. Playing the early instrument, which is different in many respects from the modern instrument on which the musician earns his living, exposes the slightest weakness of

[1] See also the *Mendelssohn* units, A100, 27–8, Section 6.

A Music Party on the Thames, by Zoffany
(Courtesy of Mrs Olive Lloyd-Baker)

intonation. As far as reading and practice make it possible, the modern player has to learn the style of playing that musicians had at the time the music he plays was composed.

Even assuming all the musicians in such a Baroque music group succeeded in capturing the spirit and style of an eighteenth-century piece of music, we cannot be sure they would sound just as they would have done in the eighteenth century. As I said earlier, very, very few stringed instruments escaped being subjected to the neck and bassbar operation in the early nineteenth century. Violins and cellos in their original condition are consequently extremely rare. A Baroque music group in which all the members have succeeded in getting original instruments sounds quite unlike anything with which we are familiar today. And, since all these instruments have now reached an age of from two hundred to two hundred-and-fifty, they will not sound exactly as they did when they were new. To hear the difference in sound between the violin as it is presently set up and the eighteenth-century instrument, one would therefore need to get a first-class maker to make both a 'modern' and an 'eighteenth-century' violin, using the same materials. The result might be illuminating.

It would simply not be true to say that all 'modern' performances of Baroque music are wrong because they do not have the smaller, eighteenth-century sound: a 'modern' performance might be far closer to the spirit and style of the period than a clinical 'authentic' performance with early instruments.

Most people are unfamiliar with the sound of the eighteenth-century instruments, and, being used to the modern, are likely to prefer that to any other. But I believe a return to the eighteenth-century sound will inevitably follow the realization that Baroque music played on modern instruments is anachronistic.

As Burney put it,[1] 'we grow nice and fastidious by frequently hearing compositions of the first class, exquisitely performed'. Our danger is that we will enjoy Corelli and Vivaldi only when exquisitely performed on modern instruments in the modern way.

Tailpiece

This brings our general introduction to the music and the instruments of the period to an end. You will be picking up these threads again—about the use and balance of orchestral forces—when you come to the Rise of the Symphony. From here, though, we go on to trace the emergence of the suite, sonata and concerto, which were the most important Baroque forms of composition: first gaining greater familiarity with the musical illustrations provided on record as we put them in a historical context, and then examining these pieces with a view to appreciating more fully how they are constructed.

[1] In the introductory 'Essay on Musical Criticism' in *BH*, ii, 11.

Abbreviations

Works to which reference is frequently made are abbreviated as follows:

AV   W. Kolneder, *Antonio Vivaldi, his life and work*, Faber and Faber, London, 1970.

BH   Charles Burney, *A General History of Music* (1789), Dover Publications Inc., New York, 1957.

BR   Hans T. David & Arthur Mendel (eds.), *The Bach Reader*, J. M. Dent & Sons Ltd., London, revised ed. 1966.

HH   Sir John Hawkins, *A General History of the Science and Practice of Music* (1776), Dover Publications Inc., New York, 1963.

HVP   David D. Boyden, *The History of Violin Playing*, Oxford University Press, London, 1965.

MBE   Manfred F. Bukofzer, *Music in the Baroque Era*, J. M. Dent & Sons Ltd., London, 1948.

MI   A. Baines (ed.), *Musical Instruments through the Ages*, Penguin Books Ltd., Harmondsworth, 1961.

NDM   Arthur Jacobs, *A New Dictionary of Music*, Penguin Books Ltd., Harmondsworth, 1958.

NOM   John Wilson (trans. and ed.), *Roger North on Music*, Novello and Co. Ltd., London, 1959.

SBE   William S. Newman, *The Sonata in the Baroque Era*, University of North Carolina Press, Chapel Hill, revised ed. 1966.

SRMH   *Source Readings in Music History*. Selected and annotated by Oliver Strunk, W. W. Norton & Co. Inc., New York, 1950.

TBC   A. J. B. Hutchings, *The Baroque Concerto*, Faber and Faber, London, 1961.

TS   H. Beck, *The Suite*, Arno Volk-Verlag, Cologne, 1964.